THE ATTIC COOKBOOK

Gertrude Wilkinson comes from upstate New York. Her father, a newspaper editor and a leading citizen of his community, always invited visiting celebrities to dinner, and it was in her parents' house that Miss Wilkinson first learned about the pleasure people take in eating. Everything there was homemade, from turtle soup to tutti-frutti. As she says, "My *Attic Cookbook* has an honorable heritage." A former food editor of the New York *Journal-American*, Miss Wilkinson is the author of many other books and articles on European and American cuisine. She has studied at the Chef's School in Madrid and at the Cordon Bleu in Paris, and from the British Museum to her grandmother's attic, she has searched for old recipes.

The
Attic Cookbook

BY GERTRUDE WILKINSON

PENGUIN BOOKS INC · BALTIMORE, MARYLAND

Grateful acknowledgement is made to the following au-
thorities, organizations and institutes:
American Spice Trade Association, Licensed Beverage In-
dustry, McCormick & Company, Inc., National Brewing
Company, Nestlé Chocolate Company, Chocolate In-
formation Council, Pan-American Coffee Bureau, Sugar
Association, Inc., Tea Council of the United States of
America, Wine Institute of California and Wine Primer
(Robert Jay Misch).

Contents

Contents

Introduction

The study and perusal of old cookbooks fascinate many men and women of the twentieth century. There are a number of diverse reasons for this lively interest in the culinary mysteries of the past. Many readers find refreshing the oddities of the old receipts, account books and menus. Others find amusing and entertaining the admonitions and exhortations that writers of bygone years laid down for their readers. Others find old cookbooks a source of astonishing facts about the early years, such as the distinction made between the better food for the so-called "upper" classes and the food that was hailed as "being good for the poor." And everyone, no matter what his other interests, has a feeling almost of awe in reading of the endurance and stamina of the early peoples. These ancient records bring to life, in the most vivid fashion, the customs, habits, dress and food of the early centuries. And for these precious fragmentary records, modern man owes the deepest debt of gratitude to the thoughtful men and women who painstakingly recorded and kept accounts of their way of life. For it is only from the treasures of the past that our knowledge of the lives of the peoples who inhabited the earth before our day has come.

The word "fragmentary" is the most applicable to use to

describe these records, for no matter what is discovered and unearthed by the scholars and historians of today, their findings are indeed far from whole. The earliest cookbook which has been handed down to us is invariably described as fragmentary. This book, about which controversy has raged for twenty centuries, is *The Art of Cooking* by Apicius. Accounts about this book vary widely. One account states that it was written by a Roman gourmet, Marcus Gabius Apicius, a man who spent the larger part of his fortune on great feasts, and when he could no longer afford them took poison. This little tale has been denied by later writers. It is known that Apicius was one of several Roman bonvivants and gastronomes in the first century, A.D.

Later writers wrote that Apicius ran a "kind of cooking school." Interest in the book, no matter who the author, or authors, were, has never died down. It was published again and again, translated into Italian and German. But it was not until the twentieth century that two translations of the Latin appeared in English. The most recent one affirms that the book was "preserved in two ninth-century manuscripts. . . . Apart from these manuscripts, some excerpts—made by a certain Vinidarius in the fifth or sixth century—have survived in an eighth-century manuscript." "It is obvious," the writer continues, "that the book we have before us is a fourth- or fifth-century edition."

However, in the twentieth century, we are not as interested in the long and tangled accounts of the book as we are entranced by the English translation of the old receipts and the knowledge we glean of the continuity of the history of our food. For from this translation it is learned that the Romans used our own familiar herbs and spices. They had honey, many familiar meats, fish, oysters, vegetables. Wines, both red and white, were used freely. The fruits of early Rome were a great delicacy and much appreciated.

Introduction

The Romans liked sweets. A favorite dessert was prepared from dates stuffed with nutmeats and fried in honey, thickened with safflower. Fresh figs were preserved in honey. A spiced wine was prepared for the benefit of travelers, because it kept forever.

These fragmentary bits and pieces of knowledge would have remained just bits and pieces forever, but in the late nineteenth century the archeologists explored and unearthed the ancient village of Pompeii. It had lain buried under the dust of centuries since the eruption of Mount Vesuvius in 79 A.D. had totally destroyed the entire village.

News of the great find excited the entire world of scholars, historians, writers and scientists. For here, in actuality was absolute proof of the way life was lived so many centuries in the past. Whole buildings were unearthed: a tavern, a bake shop, homes and shops. Household goods, home furnishings, eating and cooking utensils saw the sunlight. And there were foodstuffs: flagons of wine, jars of honey, packets of spices, dried figs, dates and kernels of wheat, corn and lentils were among the culinary treasures.

The discovery swept away all conjecture about the past; abstruse arguments were useless. The truth lay revealed for all to see. And as the knowledge became more and more general, as each succeeding generation studied the wealth of material, so did the earlier books and records become of more intense interest.

The precise date at which the renaissance of interest in the old records and cookbooks began is not known with any degree of accuracy. But it is certain from numerous historical references that the subject has always been one of lively research.

And, luckily, there are many treasures from the past from which to learn about the details of cooking and dining.

Carefully guarded records describe the great Gild (Guild) feasts of the fourteenth, fifteenth and sixteenth centuries. One such account book has the menu for the Feast of the Gild of the Holy Cross held in the fifteenth century. The menu included seven sheep and ten calves, vast quantities of ale and sugar (sugar at today's currency rates was $2.00 a pound).

Another account book of the same period depicts the day's menus in a London household. Dinner (served at 11:00 A.M.) consisted of a "pece of bief, a loyne of veal, two chickens and oranges." Supper (served at 5:30 P.M.) was simpler, with "a shoulder of mutton, 2 rabbettes, a dressing ye mutton and a piggie pettie toes."

These odd accounts are verified in other records of the past. The late fourteenth century and the early fifteenth century were rich in the old lore. One of the most famous records was The Forme of Cury. This was a vellum roll of over two hundred recipes, dating back to the year 1390.

With the advent of the printing press, the volumes began to increase. The first cookbook to be printed (in 1475) was entitled *De Honesta Voluptate*.

Soon the stream of books became a flood which has never ceased. A tiny little book, *The English Hus-Wife*, appeared in 1623. Then early in the next century, a book was published, *The Art of Cookery*, with the charming receipt for a dessert which required "one quarte of cream, two quartes of rose petals and honey mixed with other ingredients."

But shortly thereafter the lesser volumes were overshadowed by the discovery of a great treasure: the collection of 8000 volumes and 14,000 manuscripts formed by the first Earl of Oxford, Lord Harley, and his son, Sir Edward Harley. The British government was quick to realize the value of this discovery and purchased it for the British Museum for £10.000 in the year 1753. The volumes seem to have lain undisturbed in the museum's attic until the year 1888. At this time the Early English Text Society edited the entire lot of volumes, titled *The Harleian Library*.

And so, for the first time, an immensely valuable collection of books of the early Middle English period was made available to students and scholars of each generation. One of the editors devoted his talents to the culinary arts, and inscribed this foreword in one of the volumes: "The receipts would astonish modern cooks, but with the exception of the seasonings, (which are offensive to modern palates), medieval bread, rice, custards, and puddings differ in no respect from ours, the same is true of fruit pancakes, fritters. But in flavour, all was confusion."

The book's receipt for apple fritters, given below, confirms the editor's statement concerning the similarity of its receipts to those used in his day. Indeed they have many similarities to those used even into the twentieth century.

Appelles Frittours

Take yolkes of egges, draw hem through a straynour, caste there-to-faire-flour berne and ale; stere it togitre til it be thik. Make pared appelles, cut hem thyn like obleies, lay hem in be batur; ben put hem into a frying pan, and fry hem in faire grece or buttur til ben browne yelowe, then put hem in disshes, and stree sugur on hem ynogh, and serve hem forthe.

Shortly after the superb find of the Harleian books and the furore the discovery made in London, a new star was born across the English Channel in Paris. This was the birth of Brillat-Savarin (b. 1755–d. 1826). He was educated to be a lawyer, but he is remembered by every figure in the culinary arts for his book, *The Physiology Of Taste*. It is still regarded as the bible of culinary reference.

The publication of this book signaled the beginning of the golden age of great chefs de cuisine, the genuises who changed the food ideas of the civilized world. One of the first greats was Carême; born a waif, he climbed to the top of his profession and was known for his elaborate architecturally-designed confections in pastry. This was their correct nomenclature, Carême insisted. Prior to his day, cookery was regarded as belonging to Medicine—many cookbook writers were physicians to royalty.

Carême was known for many things; he wrote that Roman cooking was barbaric and that men who knew nothing of cookery insisted on writing cookbooks. He was a jealous man, but had many admirers among the members of royalty. They were fond of saying that Carême was the cook of kings and the king of cooks. He spent his entire professional life in the kitchens of royalty and near-royalty.

But he was also a charitable man and trained other chefs under him, who went on to their own glory. However, no matter how famous his successors were, each one was diminished when the great Escoffier (1846–1935) made his debut on the scene.

Escoffier owes his fame to the invitation of the Directors of the new Savoy Hotel in London (built in 1896) to direct its kitchens. The diva, Madam Melba, was residing at the new hotel and Escoffier created the now classic dessert, Pêche Melba in her honor. After his sojourn at the Savoy, Escoffier moved on to the new Carlton, which now added its name to the roster of great hotels. And it was at a banquet at the new Carlton that the Emperor of Germany, William II, said to Escoffier, "I am the Emperor of Germany but you are the Emperor of cooks."

But while Escoffier was basking in the fame that was rightfully his, in Paris another chef de cuisine was also laboring to make a name for himself. This was Jules Gouffé, a man who did not suffer from any sense of false modesty. After he had become known as a great chef, he compiled a book of his best recipes and introduced the collection as being the very first book to be written based on the author's personal experience.

As Gouffé was obliged to find a worthy explanation for many of his old recipes, he seized upon the idea that it was not retrogressive to borrow from the past that which was good. In any case, Gouffé's fame was soon overshadowed by the arrival upon the culinary scene of the incomparable César Ritz, whose great hotels are known to every worldwide traveler of this century.

But the golden days of the great chefs no longer dominated the field of cookery. Times changed too rapidly and too drastically. Today the world of haute cuisine is known to but a relatively few, and the modern demand for easily prepared meals, ready-to-eat foods, barbecues and pizzas is an enormous factor in our economy that must be reckoned with. But these matters do not take into account the inborn creative skills common to human nature that must be given expression.

Nor do modern, efficient marketing methods take under advisement the secret touch of nostalgia that lurks in every adult's heart. Many an adult speaks longingly of the days of her childhood: her visits to Grandma's house and the exploration of the big old attic, with its brass-bound trunk. Many a grown woman remembers the yellowed white satin wedding dress Grandma wore, the crumpled kid gloves, beaded purse and silk shawls. Other adults remember the old trunk crammed with hand-written receipts marked as "Aunt Nelly's Sally Lunns. Good" or "Aunt Harriet's Tutti-Frutti. Delicious."

And what adult can forget the platters of sweetened

strawberries which, covered with mosquito net, were placed in the attic to cook in the hot sunshine and hot air and which yielded Sun-Cooked Strawberries to pour over cool vanilla pudding?

But with the destruction of the rambling old houses went the destruction of the old ways and the old-time foods that required hours of time in preparation. This was "progress," we were informed.

And while it is true that today's young housekeeper is well versed in the culinary arts, and no longer cooks "spin-age" (spinach) for two hours, nor boils cabbage for an hour and a half, neither does she spend six months in the preparation of homemade vinegar. Neither does the modern housekeeper buy whole hams to hang for a month or two in a damp place to make them moldy, and then 'ty' them on a hook in a dry place.

But she does roast beef and lamb to retain the juices and reduce the shrinkage. She panbroils instead of frying in heavy fat. And she does serve well-balanced nutritious meals, with the proper quota of protein, carbohydrates, fats and sugar needed for growth and maintainence of bodily needs.

It is true our new housewives no longer have time "to beat the frosting one way for one hour," nor to "cream butter with the hand or a wooden spoon for half an hour." But she is not obliged to. For in this area, as well as in all others, manual labor has been replaced by automatic electric devices.

Furthermore, her ultramodern kitchen range, either gas or electric, offers an oven with a thermostatic heat-control device which has eliminated guesswork in baking. So it is little wonder the young housewife enjoys turning back the pages of the old receipts and trying her hand at Aunt Nelly's Sally Lunns and other good things.

Introduction

It is with pleasure this book is dedicated to Grandma's great grandchildren and great nieces, with the hope the updated, measured recipes yield many a good muffin, cake, tart, ice cream and apple pie. For "It is not retrogressive to borrow from the past that which is good."

Oddities and Admonitions of Early Writers

In today's sophisticated era the admonitions and exhortations of the early cookbook writers sound strange, but they allow for many an hour of enjoyable reading.

No modern writer would dare to lay down the law, as did the writers of the previous centuries. Following the publication of the Harleian manuscript with its foreword, writers appeared on every hand and expressed their opinions freely.

One of the first writers, Gervase Markham, who is now regarded as one of the best of the early writers, had this to say: "To speak then of the outward and active knowledges which belong to our English housewife, I hold the first and most principal to be, perfect skill and knowledge in Cookery, together with all the secretes belonging to the same, because it is a duty belonging to women . . . To sum up, She must have a quick eye, a curious nose, and a ready ear, and perfect taste."

The English gentlemen were loyal to their country's cooking if the job were carried out by a man. One of the sixteenth-century males wrote, "Cookery, in England, when well done, is superior to that of any country in the world."

The same writers were exceedingly critical of women cookbook writers, however. One of the best known writers was Hannah Glasse. Her book is available to modern readers, and today's readers will enjoy the introduction which is as follows: "This book far exceeds any Thing of the Kind yet published. By a Lady." But her detractors flatly stated it must have been written by a man.

The introduction in Mrs. Glasse's book is not the only enjoyable bit to read. Her receipt for a pie crust (1747) reads: "For a cold cruft, take three Pounds of Flour, a Pound and a Half of Butter, two eggs and cold water. Beat the Pastry with a Rolling Pin." Devotees of southern beaten biscuits will find in this recipe a very familiar sound.

Modern cooks will find the receipt from "a Prudent Housewife" for a Cherry Tart as simple to follow as today's recipe: "Take two Pounds of Cherries, bruife, ftone and ftamp them. And boil up their juice with sugar; then ftone four Pounds more of Cherries, and put them into your Tart with the Cherry Syrup, bake your Tart, ice it and serve it up." However there is a genuine difference in icing a tart. The old cookbooks instruct their readers to draw a feather across the tart, after dipping the feather in the icing.

In browsing through a number of the old books, the reader will often note a striking similarity in the attitude of each generation concerning the wastefulness and extravagance of previous generations. In one of the earlier books written in the nineteenth century, one male writer was indignant over the receipts printed by his predecessors. He assured *his* readers they would find no receipts for venison boiled in wine, nor for roasted whole peacocks. His philosophy, he stated, was to print a practical book.

But another writer threw thrift to the winds. In a delightful book, printed at the opening of the nineteenth century, *Warner's Antiquitates Culinarise*, appears a receipt for a French Cake, to eat hot, that required the use of a dozen eggs, a "quarte" of cream, a pound of butter, and, for the liquid, the gentleman selected a bottle of white wine.

However, receipts and housekeeping were not the only topics discussed in old cookbooks. One writer sternly admonished her readers not to let their children romp away their existence and wear out their good clothes. Instead, they could profitably spend their time picking blackberries to sell at six cents a quart.

There were even some eighteenth-century writers who concentrated on Household Hints and included no receipts. One such writer, concerned about the need for thrift, advised the laundress to dip silk handkerchiefs and dark blue factory cotton in salt water to prevent fading.

Even in the South, where the great bounty of the fields, streams and orchards provided luxurious meals, thrift was regarded as highly important. A famous writer of her day, Mary Randolph Washington, was exceedingly firm in her dictum that early rising was an absolute necessity. How, she sensibly inquired, could the mistress of the household expect her slaves or servants to carry out their duties, with no supervision? In New England, an early writer, Maria Parloa, was insistent that an immense income was not essential to live well.

For farm dwellers, one writer offered counsel for cold weather: "If cold weather is apprehended, the pump handle should be set as high as possible, and a horse blanket thrown over it." Other writers worried about unexpected company and urged the young housewife to keep a piece of calf's rennet soaking in wine. By this means, a dessert could be prepared in a matter of minutes.

Thrift, keeping house, doing the laundry, watching the servants, being a hostess—all played their part in the early cookbooks. The writers even included advice "for keeping hair clean and shining, use New England rum."

There was still another striking difference between the older cookbooks and the new. The writers took no note of seemliness. Directions for Medicine for Canary Birds would immediately precede a recipe for Caramel Candies. This recipe was followed by a thrifty substitute for cream for coffee. The idea was simplicity itself. "Beat the white of an egg to a froth, add a small lump of butter and," concludes the writer, "no one can tell the difference."

And for housewives who lived on farms, one writer explained how to keep cherries fresh for an entire year, by simply packing them in alternate layers of hay, shutting them up in an airtight keg and keeping the keg warm in the chimney corner."

Unlike the modern housewife who can run to the store for her slightest wish, the early housewife had to be fully prepared and to make do with what she had. Very often for cakes and pies and puddings of divers sorts all she had to use were whole spices: allspice, cloves, cinnamon, nutmeg. If the whole spice did not suit her purpose, she could prepare a tincture of the spice in about two weeks time. This technique involved the "bruising" of the spice, pouring a quart of brandy over a three-ounce quantity of a single spice. At the end of the fortnight, the liquid was poured off and a spoonful or two used as needed. One cookbook author concludes: "A spoonful of tincture of cinnamon in a glass of sherry wine is a very exhilarating cordial."

Not only were the old cookbooks replete with receipts for cooking fresh foods; they also included elaborate instructions for drying beans, corn, apples, peaches, pears. Instructions on salting down fresh green beans and preserving eggs throughout the long winter were also explained.

If the housewife followed the instructions given so freely, she could have home made corn beef, smoked ham and bacon, potted meats, onions, carrots, squash and pumpkins all winter long. Barrels of apples and potatoes were too customary to need any information about storage.

Many of the books gave details for setting the table for breakfast, luncheon, a Gentleman's Dinner Party, A Lady's Informal Tea. The menu in each instance was an astonishing array of food, the most remarkable being the foods served at the Lady's Tea. There were raw oysters, cabbage salad, pickled crab apples, broiled chicken, creamed potatoes, hot biscuits. Charlotte Russe, Pattycakes and Lemon Jelly Cake completed the repast. So rich and elaborate were the menus of the nineteenth century that it is hard to believe that foods of such variety and in such astonishing amounts were actually served.

But the effect of technological changes on cookery was already being noted. An English cookbook, written in the very middle of the nineteenth century, states: "Why, intercommunication between distant nations has become so facile and frequent, it is possible to enjoy a very early breakfast in London and a very late dinner in Paris. Therefore, cookery cannot remain stationery."

Our Daily Bread
Then and Now

The origin of wheat has been traced as far back as the Neolithic Man (6000–7000 B.C.) and is said to be the oldest cereal cultivated by man. When the grain was ground into flour and baked into a loaf of bread, it is known to have been the principal article of diet for centuries in many areas of the world.

From the earliest days, when primitive man scratched the surface of the earth with a sharp pointed stick, to the days of the first clumsy, awkward farm tools, ploughing, planting, reaping, and harvesting the grain was a backbreaking monumental task.

Then the wheat had to be separated from the chaff and ground into flour. With the coming of the first gristmills, the grain was ground between enormous stone wheels by the method the modern miller calls "the one-step sudden death" grinding.

During all these aeons, little appreciable change was seen in the cultivation of grain until the early 1880's. And then changes occurred with great rapidity, completely altering methods of farming and the subsequent quality of the milled grains.

But until then, the method of milling left great quantities of powdered husks in the flour. And when the bags or barrels of flour reached the housewife's kitchen, the husks had to be sifted out as best it could. The tool for this chore was a crude, clumsy sieve, known as a Tammy.

As the cookbooks began to appear, the writers offered advice and counsel on the purchase and use of the flour. As one writer stated, "If, after trying a barrel of flour twice, you find it becomes wet and sticky, it is better to return it."

Another writer spoke up and said, "The best method to pursue in buying flour is, first, to find a good dealer upon whose advice you may rely. Next, take a sample of the flour recommended to you and with a receipt which you have *proved* to be correct, try some. If the first loaf of bread is not satisfactory, try another and then another, until you are confident that the fault lies in the flour and not in the method of baking. Finally, having found a brand of flour . . . which feels elastic to the hand, keep it; it is probably good. It is just as easy to have good bread as poor."

Another of the authors was quite emphatic in her beliefs. "In my opinion, poor bread I consider an unnecessary article to have in the home."

But poor flour was not the only worry for the housewives of earlier times. One writer offered this bit of information. "Baking with yeast and/or cream of tartar and soda are the two most practical methods of baking bread. But the difficulty of obtaining good cream of tartar is very great. It is said to be more extensively adulterated than any other food." Measuring the ingredients was also important. "A fairly accurate measure may be obtained," continues the writer "by measuring a teaspoon of each, (cream of tartar and soda) in exactly the same manner and then taking a little off the soda."

There were other problems, as well. Yeast had to be prepared and there were many receipts for that task, depending upon whether the yeast was to be Barm-Yeast or Ale Yeast.

The fact that despite all these problems excellent bread was baked is pointed out by an English parson who said, "Of bread made of wheat we have sundry sorts daily brought to the table, whereof the first and most excellent is the Manchet, which we commonly call white bread."

The old cookbooks described the early English fireplaces and bake ovens. The food was cooked, either by being "seethed" or roasted over a "spit." The oven was of brick and the baking of bread and all manner of cakes was done once a week.

The stone exterior of the oven was semicircular in shape, and was generally built at the gable end of the Old World cottages. Opposite the door of the oven a large, light-colored stone was built into the wall; this served the purpose of a rude thermometer, changing color with the degree of heat induced as the carbon burned away, leaving the stone glowing at a white heat against its blacker neighbors. A shutter called a "Stopless" closed the oven door.

But the structure and character of the equipment of the Old World did not remain static. Each new generation made improvements over the "old ways" until by the 1800's the kitchen and the kitchen fireplace were "the heart of the home." A recently published book, *Home, Sweet Home*, describes the fireplace and oven of the nineteenth century as follows:

"It was the most important fireplace in the house; it was also the most complicated and the biggest, maybe four feet deep, seven feet high, ten feet wide. . . . and it was kept blazing all day and often glowing at night, all year round."

On the pavement inside the great hearth, there stood two sturdy andirons, set maybe six feet apart, to hold the main logs. Bolted to one side of the stone fireplace perhaps five feet above the hearthstone was a heavy wrought-iron crane which could be swung in over the flames or swung away from them to hang or remove the pots and kettles.

It was a very fortunate housewife who owned a fireplace with a built-in oven. But lacking such a luxury, she could still bake, that is, she could cook with indirect confined heat by using a Dutch oven, buried deep in the ashes on the hearth.

But as the housewife struggled with her problems—poor flour, adulterated cream of tartar, uneven and temperamental ovens—she also fought a losing battle with the old-time, often inaccurate receipts. For in contrast to today's briskly efficient recipes, the old receipts called for a heaping cup of this, a scant cup of that, enough cayenne pepper to cover a silver dollar, a lump of butter the size of a black walnut.

Basically the receipts were the same. But not in all cases. The Ash Cake, as it was known in Old Virginia, stemmed, historians state, from the first bread or cake, known as a Bannock (today a delicious bun). It was said to be the cake that King Alfred allowed to burn up in the fire as he sat brooding in the peasant's cottage.

As the number of cookbooks increased, so did the number of receipts, which were given names that sound quaint to us in the twentieth century. There were Huffkins, Chudleighs, Whigs, Cobs, Pikelets, Singin Hinnies, Hawkshaws and Girdles. As the receipts changed for the better, so did some of the names. Pikelets became Crumpets; Singin Hinnies became Scones and in many instances were renamed Girdle Cakes. (And our modern griddle originally, of course, was Girdle.)

And as each century passed into history, so did each branch of culinary art change—in many instances for the better, but not always. But the coarse, yellowish flour improved; yeast improved; and cooking methods improved.

Probably the greatest single change that affected future cookery was the improved milled flour. The old-time millers ground the flour between huge millstones. Modern millers employ a "Reduction" method—a highly technical, complicated step-by-step technique that yields seventy-two percent of the original grain, thus producing the extreme refined white flour we have today.

If a larger percentage of the grain were milled, the result would be a darker flour, unacceptable by today's standards, which call for the removal of the wheat germ. The wheat germ is sold separately, and the white loaf is "enriched" by vitamins and minerals.

Thus modern nutrition is served by these extensive manufacturing processes and today's housewife finds a great variety of flours available for her selection. Modern plant research and plant breeding has given the twentieth-century housewife the most luxurious wheat and other grain products.

There are just two basic types of flour, but there are many varieties. Winter wheat, or *hard* wheat, is rich in gluten which yields the necessary elasticity for making bread. Spring wheat, or *soft* wheat, is used for making pastries, cakes, and baked goods of all sorts. Whole wheat (graham flour) is used for a variety of breads and muffins, sometimes singly, but more often in combination with white flour.

The other important grains—rye, oats and corn—are used for all manner of breads, muffins, waffles, pancakes and rolls. Corn is converted into cornmeal for breads, cakes and puddings.

From Fireplace to Electronic Range

The story of fire and man's use of it has been documented from the earliest days of primitive man right through the centuries up to and including our own. Every school child is familiar with the pictures of the clay tablets which depict man crouched over a fire, cooking over the blaze a piece of meat impaled on a long pointed stick.

Every tale about the first cooked meal concerns the poor peasant whose dwelling burned down and who, as he searched among the embers, came upon his well-roasted little pig, and, burning and sucking his fingers, tasted roast pork. But this tale, pleasing though it is, has no authenticity. More creditable accounts describe man's burying a pot of food in the embers of a fire and heaping hot ashes over the pot.

Heavy iron pots were used extensively in the earlier centuries when fireplaces were the only means of cooking food, and many an American attic revealed Grandma's collection of sturdy, three-legged iron pots, or Dutch ovens, as they were often called. As recently as the nineteenth century, the Irish people baked bread on the hearth, the pot well covered with peat.

And so it came about that after centuries of primitive cooking methods, in the nineteenth century the inventive mind of man began to bloom forth with new methods of cooking food. The first coal and wood range was a landmark in releasing the housewife from sheer drudgery. This revolutionary change began with the first shipment of coal ranges to the New World by Scandanavian emigrants early in the 1800's. They had been originally designed as heaters and were called, appropriately, Norse Heaters.

Immediately upon their installation in American households, American ironmongers and blacksmiths began to experiment with the clumsy things. But they labored for many decades before their work resulted in the first coal and wood range for cooking. One would ordinarily suppose that such a miraculous invention would take the country by storm. But the truth was that the early manufacturers had a hard time to obtain popular acceptance.

And, as manufacturers are obliged to advertise their wares today, so did the early manufacturers of the coal and wood ranges. The earliest of the advertisements stressed the advantages of the range over the old fireplace. They explained that the heat was contained within the stove; therefore, it was less wasteful. And since the heat was contained, cooking was faster and more convenient. Finally, it was much safer than a fireplace.

Soon more and more models made their appearance and more and more advertisements followed. One such commercial read, "To surpass all others for economy in fuel and dispatch in cooking." Another ad extravagantly claimed the Simpson Stove to be: "An elegant piece of furniture for parlor when not needed for cooking."

But in spite of all the publicity and advertising the coal stove did not attain any real popularity until Millard Fillmore took office and ordered a huge coal and wood stove for the White House kitchens. But he was met with outraged indignation on the part of the cooks. They took off their aprons, stormed out of the kitchens, exclaiming, "This new-fangled contraption." The poor President was obliged to call in an expert from the United States Patent Office to explain the intricacies of the stove to the cooks.

But by the beginning of the Civil War, the ownership of a coal range was a mark of social status. And as the "new-fangled" stove won acceptance, the manufacturers added new improvements. They included a trough to hold hot water, an oven for baking, removable stove lids and cooking "plates" of varying sizes.

Ownership of a coal range began to be accepted as a matter of course. New factors added their weight to the use of coal and the displacement of wood. New and vast coal mines were opened up, bringing the price of coal down to the reach of the average family, although the rural areas were still dependent on wood stoves.

But coal was not to maintain its supremacy for long. Natural gas was known and used as an illuminant and the same inventive type of mind that was responsible for so many of the new devices of the nineteenth century began to work on using gas as a fuel for cooking.

The first patents dealt with a two-burner gas plate, but it was not much better than a hot plate and it made little impression on the housewives in the 1830's. But the zealous inventors and manufacturers continued with their improvements and in the year 1866 the first patent for a gas stove was issued.

The next few years, after centuries of using the hearth and fireplace for cooking, were marked by rapid changes and innovations.

Writers of cookbooks were very quick to take cognizance of the changes, not only with their updated receipts for cooking with coal, but also with their reams of advice on housekeeping. "Store-bought" bread was still regarded as inferior to the homemade loaf and the writers did not hesitate to say so.

Just as in earlier days, the temperature of the oven was a temperamental thing and the writers explained how to test the heat of the oven of the coal stove. One writer advised using a sheet of white paper and keeping an eye on it. If it reached a pale yellow, it was good for cake; it it reached a deep yellow, it was right for bread. Or, "The oven should be just hot enough that the hand can bear the heat."

As "hot breads" for breakfast were customary, the housewife was advised to "attend to the fire; see that you have a clear, steady one."

When young housekeepers, accustomed to the hearths of their mothers and grandmothers, were faced with the new iron monster in their first home, the writers rushed to her aid with voluminous instructions. One book, in instructions headed *What To Do In The Morning*, prescribed the following: "First, make the kitchen fire; take up and sift the ashes. After brushing all the dust from the range, wash off the surface with a cloth and soap and water; then polish it with stove blacking. Rinse out the teakettle, and after the water has been running from the cold-water pipes for five minutes, fill the kettle and place it on the fire. Sweep and dust the kitchen. Put the breakfast dishes on to heat. Air the dining room and set the table. *Then* prepare and serve the breakfast."

As if these orders were not enough, the new housewife had to be an expert in her choice of coffee beans. For her coffee was a blend of different coffee beans. The gourmets of the period wrote that two-thirds of Mocha coffee beans and one-third Java was the most superior blend.

The purchase of the beans was followed by grinding the coffee each morning in the "new" French coffee grinder. There were two recognized methods of preparing the brew.

The method still regarded as best was the drip method in an earthenware or china biggin (no metal). The other more common method of the nineteenth century was boiled coffee.

If the coffee was boiled, then the grounds had to "settle." For this purpose a crushed egg shell was dropped into the pot at the last minute. Another method was to add an unshelled egg to the cold water and let the egg boil with the coffee. Still another writer suggested that a small piece of salt fish skin be boiled with the coffee (to make the brew perfectly clear).

Breakfasts were gargantuan meals. If buckwheat cakes were on the menu, the old earthenware pitcher of the batter was brought from the ice-cold pantry to warm up. The pot of oatmeal cereal was kept on the back of the stove all night and brought forward to heat in the morning. Orange juice? Unheard of in the nineteenth century. Half-oranges were served, but as a great treat for Sunday breakfast.

A TYPICAL BREAKFAST MENU
FROM THE YEAR 1880 A.D.

Either oatmeal or hominy should always be served at breakfast. When it is possible, have fruit for the first course.

Fruit

Oatmeal and Cream

Baked potatoes   Mutton Chops   Rye Muffins

Hominy Griddle Cakes

Coffee, Tea or Chocolate

The other meals of the day were on the same order of quantity. But as the years advanced and the inventors of new appliances continued to pour out their beneficence on the American public and farm life slowly gave way to urban life, the quantity of food served began to diminish.

With the advent of the gas range, the popularity of the coal range began to fade. Writers now began to issue directions for cleaning the gas range, sensibly admonishing housewives not to use stove blacking but to rub daily inside and out with a cloth dipped in olive oil.

Various designs in gas ranges continued to be turned out by the gas companies, but the problem of exact baking time continued to plague everyone until, in the year 1913, the most significant change in the history of cooking took place. Oven heat control devices appeared on the new ranges.

A story accompanies the new and wonderful invention.

It seems that many long years ago a farm boy watched his mother's distress when her bread burned. He took a vow that when he grew up he would invent a gadget to prevent such things happening. The boy grew up and became an executive in a company which invented a thermostat for a water heater. And, lo, the oven thermostat was born.

But fame lasts briefly. Very shortly the wonder of the new gas range was fading from the attention of the fickle public. For now the first electric range made its appearance. Inventors had been tinkering with this idea since the year 1896, and some experimental notes stated that such an appliance had been designed in 1859.

The first electric range must have been a simple design, for the writers stated that it operated as a telephone switchboard, with every pot and pan plugged in separately. But in the first decade of the 20th century, the modern electric range, familiar to all of today's housekeepers, was designed, and installed in homes across the nation. At the time the experts stated, "This is the ultimate in design."

But they were wrong, for as the 1900's passed the halfway

mark the first electronic range was placed on exhibit in New York City. The audience was invited to watch a five-pound roast cook perfectly in thirty minutes, a pan of hot muffins in three minutes. But experienced salesmen did not worry, for the initial price of the electronic range was $1200.00.

But our story of the fireplace and hearth to the electronic range cannot come to an end without remarking on the twin revolutionary development of the modern refrigerator, which swept the old wooden iceboxes out of homes across the nation. The first modest Monitor Top electric refrigerator appeared in 1927, and, like a host of other inventions, new and more elaborate refrigerator and freezing appliances have continued to be built ever since.

A gas refrigerator was designed and sold in the first quarter of the 1900's, but the manufacture of the electric freezer far outclassed the former and it quietly faded from the scene.

Today's housewives may reflect that never before in the history of mankind has the average family enjoyed so much luxury, so much ease and convenience in keeping house, cleaning the house, storing the food, preparing and cooking the food, nor paid so much for it all.

Sweetenings of Early Days

The history of the sweetenings we consume in the twentieth century is the history of civilization itself. Modern manufacturing methods have refined the crude original foods but the characteristic flavor and sweetness of each one is the same today as it was centuries ago.

The sap of the maple tree was known to early man and sugar cane was chewed directly from the stalk. Honey is mentioned repeatedly in the Old Testament.

When the early settlers reached the New World, they brought hives of bees along with them, which the Indians named "White Men's flies." Contrary to popular opinion, bees were not indigenous to the American shores. It is thought by historians that the bees escaped from the hives, and thus began the consumption of wild honey.

However, this was not the case with maple syrup. Maple trees were indigenous on this side of the Atlantic and the early settlers were prompt in taking advantage of this unexpected find. Again, the Indians were responsible for finding a name for the colonists' discovery, and called the maple syrup "Sweet water."

As sugar was scarce and expensive, molasses soon became one of the prime ingredients in the housewife's repertoire of foods. As one historian wrote, "Colonial New England

28

is a veritable sea of rum." The Puritan New Englanders found the manufacture of rum a highly profitable enterprise. And as molasses was an essential ingredient in its manufacture, molasses was cheap and plentiful. It was shipped in enormous barrels to the local areas, where it was transferred to gallon jugs, from which it poured in a slow stream of rich, dark viscous fluid.

Today's housewife will find honey in glass jars, maple syrup in tins, and molasses in glass jars from which it flows quickly and smoothly. But in the case of the development of processing sugar, its history is a long one. As with many of our other basic foods, legends surround the history of the sugarcane. The earliest legend, a Hindu tale, relates that a "Hindu prince begged to be admitted into Heaven so that he could enjoy the paradise while he was still alive. Through shrewd dealings with a holy hermit, the Prince managed to get into the celestial palace only to be thrown out by Indra, the King of the Heavens.

"The hermit witnessed the fall, intercepted the prince and created another paradise for him midway between heaven and earth. In this paradise grew sugarcane and other delectable foods. So grateful was the prince that, later when he was accepted into heaven, he threw down the sugar cane as a gift to mortal man."

Sad to relate, this charming little fable is just that. Scholars and researchers state that undoubtedly sugar cane was indigenous to islands in the South Pacific, and from there it was carried to India and Southeast Asia through the migration of population.

The art of sugar manufacture originated in India in 600 A.D. and even earlier references to sugar cane have been traced in Buddhist literature.

Early methods were crude and simple. The juice was pressed from the cane, and boiled until solids were formed in the shape of small pebbles, *sarkara*, from which comes our word, sugar. The larger pebbles were called *khanda*, the root of our word candy.

But many centuries passed before sugar was manufactured and used as a great ingredient in cookery. It was consumed in simple form—plain hard lumps as sugar candy, or as syrup for bread, later described in cookbooks as "Sugar Sops."

The use of sugar as a sweetener was a rare luxury, and its price so enormous only royalty and the very wealthy could afford to purchase it well through the sixteenth century. As noted in the account of the great Guild Feast, sugar sold for $2.00 a pound in modern currency. The Spanish colonists introduced sugar to the New World in the late fifteenth century, but until the middle of the sixteenth century its use was still confined to the wealthy. And though used as a sweetener for sauces, it was thought of as a spice rather than a sweet.

When the working classes first heard about and began to use the new delicacy, they were "roundly condemned by their 'Betters' for this self-indulgence." However, history was on the side of the working class. For as the shrewd traders of the era learned of the great profits to be made in sugar, their freighters began to sail the seas. And as the volume of sales increased, the prices dropped. But it took a long time, up to the middle of the eighteenth century, before the drop was appreciable.

The use of sugar as a basic ingredient received its greatest impetus when coffee made its debut in the culinary world early in the 1600's. Coffee houses began to spring up everywhere in Europe and sugar was always served with the popular new beverage. By the 1700's sugar was an indispensable ingredient in the diet, just as it is today.

However, its early manufacture was a far cry from today's

refined process. Originally the sugar was pressed into cone-shaped molds, sometimes weighing from 12 to 50 pounds. The cones were suspended from the ceiling by a heavy cord, with a net over the cone to keep off the flies. (Old woodcuts show this example of early use.) The housewife had to knock off chunks as she wished to use it. Prior to the Civil War, sugar was sold in huge barrels, and it was so brown and hard it required a sugar auger to dig it out. As the industry methods improved and the quality improved, the stores carried sugar in one-hundred-pound barrels.

In the New England towns and villages, the local stores catered to the small farms which abounded in the late eighteenth century. Barter and exchange were a common and popular practice. While it is true that the farms were practically self-sufficient (before the days of the mechanized farms and the subsequent destruction of the small one-family farm), still there were some staple articles of diet the farmer could not grow.

He had to exchange homegrown foods for his supply of salt, pepper, tea, coffee, chocolate, raisins and sugar. During a period of new development in the old New England village of Danbury, Connecticut, the excavations underneath the location of an old grocery store yielded a faded sign which read as follows: "Brown sugar, Loaf sugar, lump sugar, tea, coffee, allspice, chocolate and pepper all kinds of country produce received in payment. Good rock salt exchanged for flaxseed, rye even."

The farmers' wives were thrifty women. They churned butter, grew vegetables, picked berries, kept chickens and exchanged their products for the precious commodities they couldn't grow. A common expression used by the farm women, "My butter and egg money," was heard all over New England, even as recently as the twentieth century.

Housewives purchased the precious sugar in one-hundred

pound muslin bags, which, after use, were ripped up, washed, hemmed and used as towels. The instructions in the early cookbooks, "Sift the sugar," testify to the coarseness of the sugar. Today modern methods of sugar manufacture make sifting unnecessary in most cooking.

Today's housewife will find available at every grocer's a variety of sugars unexcelled in fineness and quality—granulated sugar, superfine sugar, 10-X confectioner's sugar, light brown sugar, dark brown sugar, granulated brown sugar, cubes and tablets of loaf sugar.

And yet, while sugar is king of all the sweeteners, the old-time receipts which call for molasses, honey or maple sugar yield delicious homemade desserts and sauces.

Breads and Rolls, Muffins, Pancakes and Waffles

In no branch of cookery is the difference between the receipts of the past and the recipes of the present more marked than in the method of baking breads and rolls.

18th Century Ash Cakes

Sweep a clean place on the hottest part of the hearth. Put the cake on it and cover with the hot wood ashes. Wash and wipe it dry before eating the cake.

AFTERNOON TEA MUFFINS

1894

Preheat oven to 400°   *One dozen muffin tins*

2 cups sifted all-purpose flour
2 teaspoons double-acting baking powder
2 tablespoons sugar

½ teaspoon salt
2 eggs, well beaten
1 tablespoon butter, melted
1 cup milk

Resift flour with dry ingredients. Combine eggs, butter and milk. Add the liquids to the dry ingredients and mix very quickly. The batter will be somewhat lumpy. Fill the well-greased tins ⅔ full. Bake for 20 to 25 minutes. Let stand on cake rack for a brief minute, turn out and serve hot.

AUNT HARRIET'S TEA MUFFINS

1894

Preheat oven to 400°　　　　*Two dozen muffin tins*

2 cups sifted cake flour	½ teaspoon salt
1 pint light cream	6 egg whites
6 egg yolks, beaten until thick	½ teaspoon cream of tartar
¼ cup sugar	1 teaspoon vanilla extract

Stir flour and cream together until just blended. Add the egg yolks, sugar and salt. Stir together quickly. In separate bowl, beat egg whites until frothy. Add the cream of tartar and beat until stiff, but not dry. Fold into the batter until all pieces of egg white are absorbed. Add the flavoring. Divide evenly into buttered muffin tins. Fill tins ⅔ to ¾ full. Bake for 15 to 20 minutes. Cool on wire cake rack for just a minute. Turn out of tins and serve warm.

AUNT MARTHA'S AFTERNOON TEA MUFFINS

Preheat oven to 375°　　　　*Two dozen muffin tins*

2 eggs	1 teaspoon baking powder
1 pint sour cream	Extra flour, if needed
½ teaspoon soda	1 tablespoon mild vinegar
½ teaspoon salt	2 tablespoons melted butter
3 cups sifted all-purpose flour	1 cup chopped pecan nutmeats

Beat eggs until light and fluffy, add the cream and mix together thoroughly. Sift all dry ingredients together twice. Combine vinegar and butter. Stir all ingredients together, quickly and lightly, just enough to blend. Stir in nutmeats. If mixture is too thin (it should be a rather stiff batter), add a little of the extra sifted flour at a time. Butter the muffin tins generously. Fill ⅔ full. Bake for 15 to 20 minutes. Turn out on wire rack and serve hot.

BAKING POWDER BISCUITS

Preheat oven to 400°   *Baking pan*

2 cups sifted all-purpose flour   *¼ cup butter and lard (½ and*
2½ teaspoons baking powder   *½), firm consistency*
1 teaspoon salt   *½ to ¾ cup milk*

Resift the flour with the dry ingredients. Cut the shortening in with two knives or a pastry blender until the mixture is the consistency of coarse corn meal. Shape a well in center of the flour, add the milk all at once and stir quickly. The mixture must be stiff enough to roll out. Turn out on lightly floured board and shape the dough with your hands. Pat gently and roll out lightly. Cut into rounds and bake until golden brown, about 10 to 12 minutes, depending on the thickness of the rounds.

For a crusty biscuit, place about one inch apart in baking pan. For a typical soft biscuit texture place the biscuits close together.

BARM BRACK BREAD

1800

Preheat oven to 325°

Two 8-inch loaf pans, or
One 8-inch loaf pan and one
7-inch square pan

1 pound mixed dried fruits
(apples, pears, apricots) cut
into bits, or 1 pound raisins
1 cup dark brown sugar
1 cup strong, cold tea

1 egg, well-beaten
2 cups sifted all-purpose flour
1 teaspoon baking powder
⅛ teaspoon salt

Rinse the cut-up fruit (or raisins) in cold water. Drain well
and add sugar and tea. Cover and let stand 24 hours. Pour
off the liquid and set it aside. Add the egg to the fruit and
stir well. Add the sifted dry ingredients alternately with the
tea liquid, beginning and ending with the flour mixture.
Grease pans, line bottoms with wax paper, and oil the paper with pastry brush dipped in oil. Divide the batter between the two pans. Bake 1 hour. Invert on wire cake rack.
When completely cooled, slice in very thin slices, or just
break off pieces. Serve with tea or coffee.

BLACKBERRY BUNS

17th century
Shall the blessed sun of Heaven prove a micher and eat blackberries.

HENRY IV.

Preheat oven to 375°   *Cookie sheet*

¼ cup unsalted butter   ¾ cup sifted cake flour
¼ cup lard   ¼ cup cornstarch
½ cup sugar   1 teaspoon baking powder
1 egg, well beaten   1 egg white, unbeaten
¾ to 1 cup blackberry preserves

Cream butter and lard; add the sugar gradually and beat until light and fluffy. Add the egg and preserves, beat in thoroughly until well blended. Resift the flour with cornstarch and baking powder. Add to the batter and stir in well. Turn out on lightly floured board.

Divide into 8 portions, shape into rounds and arrange on buttered cookie sheet, or shallow baking pan, close together. Brush tops lightly with egg white. Bake for 20 minutes. Cool slightly on wire cake rack and serve warm.

BOSTON BROWN BREAD

Three 1-pound coffee tins

1 cup sifted all-purpose flour   1 cup molasses
4 cups whole wheat flour   2 cups buttermilk
1 teaspoon soda   1 cup golden raisins, sprinkled
1 teaspoon salt   lightly with flour

Mix dry ingredients together. In large bowl combine molasses and buttermilk. Mix thoroughly and gradually beat flour into the liquid. Shake excess flour from raisins and stir the raisins into the batter. Grease 3 tins, fill each tin ⅔ full. Cover tightly with lids, or tie wax paper over.
Steam for 3 hours. (See p. 171 for Directions for Steaming Foods.)
Cool on wire cake rack, removing covers immediately. Remove from tins when cool. This bread keeps well.

HOMEMADE BREAD

The weekly task of baking bread in Grandmother's day was a day's work all by itself. The directions in the notebooks were profuse. "When you put the bread on the board, pat it lightly. Do not press down . . . Do not stop kneading until you have finished. Bread which has 'rested' is not good. . . . In cold weather some kitchens grow cold very quickly after the fire is out. In this case bread should be made earlier in the evening and set in a warmer place . . . breakfast rolls are placed close together in even rows in the pan. The best sized pan for bread is made of block tin. . . . There are many kinds of bread that can be made readily and safely after once learning to make good common bread. . . . The best flour is always the cheapest for bread. . . . As there is no one article of food of so great importance, learn to make it as nearly perfect as possible.
Shaping the Loaves . . . Hold the lard in the hand until it is very soft, then rub it over the loaves."

Yeast

To make yeast at home, the poor woman had to boil potatoes, add sugar, salt, a little flour, and "water into which a small handful of hops has been boiled. . . . This will keep for months. . . . As poor yeast is the cause of poor bread, pains should be taken to make it properly and keep it well. The jug should be thoroughly washed and *scalded* each time the yeast is renewed. As much care should be taken with the stopper as with the jug."

The instructions then continue: "Cover the dough closely, that neither dust nor air can get in . . . The dough will rise in eight or nine hours. In the morning shape into loaves or rolls. Let rise an hour."

Testing the oven for the right temperature was done as follows: "Bake in an oven that will brown a teaspoon of flour in five minutes . . . Use a bit of crockery for the flour (as it will have a more even heat)."

In her book, *The Young Housekeeper* (1880), Maria Parloa, a New England writer, advises the new cook that a "piece of woolen blanket is of great value in making bread. Wrap it around the bowl in which the bread is rising. Nothing is more injurious than chilling the dough before it has risen." In this century the goodness of homemade bread can be enjoyed by methods available to every housewife. Breadmaking today is a matter of the utmost simplicity.

20th-Century Recipe for Bread

Preheat oven to 400°   *Two 9 x 6 x 3-inch loaf bread pans*

½ cup milk
3 tablespoons sugar
2 teaspoons salt
3 tablespoons butter
1½ cups warm water (105°–115°)

1 package or cake yeast, dry or compressed
5½ cups flour (about)

Scald the milk, stir in sugar, salt and butter. Cool to luke-warm. Warm another bowl, pour out the *hot* water. Pour in the warm water, sprinkle or stir the yeast over the water and stir until the yeast is dissolved. Add the lukewarm milk mixture and stir in. Add 3 cups of flour and beat until smooth. Add more flour, one-half cup at a time, enough to make a soft, but not a sticky, dough.

Turn out on lightly floured board and knead until elastic and blisters spring up (about 10 minutes). Shape between hands into smooth ball. Grease a large bowl and turn the dough until all of it is well greased. Cover, let stand in a warm place, free from drafts, until double in bulk. Punch down. Let "rest" for 15 minutes. Divide dough in half, shape each loaf and place in well-buttered bread pans. Cover, let stand in warm place, free from draft, until doubled in bulk, about 1 hour.

Bake about 30 minutes. Turn out of pans at once, brush tops with melted butter. Let cool thoroughly. When cold, may be properly wrapped and placed in freezer, if desired.

Hints on Bread-Making

1. To test the warm water for the dough, if a thermometer is lacking, drop a few drops on the inside of your wrist.

2. The milk mixture and the yeast mixture must be the same lukewarm temperature.

3. If the dough becomes sticky on the floured board, add a teaspoon of flour at a time (under the dough) and flour your hands again.

4. A good way to let the dough double in bulk is to let the bowl stand in a deep, larger bowl partially filled with warm (not hot) water.

5. To test for "double in bulk," press two fingers lightly on the dough. If the imprint of your fingers remains, the dough has doubled in bulk.

BUTTERMILK BISCUITS

Preheat oven to 375°   *9 x 13-inch baking pan*

1 pint buttermilk
1 teaspoon soda dissolved in 1
   tablespoon warm water
¼ cup melted butter

2½ to 3 cups sifted all-purpose
   flour
½ teaspoon salt

Combine the milk, soda water and butter. (Add the salt to the first cup of flour.) Add the flour gradually until the mixture is stiff enough to be rolled out and cut into rounds. Bake in a greased pan for 20 to 25 minutes. Cool slightly on cake rack and serve warm.

Variation: Sour Cream Biscuits

Substitute sour cream for the buttermilk, reduce the amount of melted butter to 2 tablespoons and add 1 tablespoon sugar.

BUTTERMILK MUFFINS

1894

Preheat oven to 400°   *One dozen muffin tins*

1½ cups sifted all-purpose
   flour
1 tablespoon sugar
½ teaspoon salt
1 cup buttermilk

½ teaspoon soda dissolved in 1
   tablespoon cold water
1 egg, well beaten
2 tablespoons melted butter

Resift flour with sugar and salt. Mix the buttermilk with the soda water and beat into the flour, stirring well. Add the egg, beat into the mixture and finally add the melted butter.

Divide evenly into greased muffin tins and bake 15 to 20 minutes. Turn out of tins and serve hot.

BUTTERMILK YEAST ROLLS

Preheat oven to 375°　　　　　*Two-inch muffin tins, or 9-inch square or round (1½-inch deep) cake pan, or cookie sheet*

2 cups buttermilk	1 teaspoon soda
1 cake compressed yeast	1½ teaspoons salt
4½ cups sifted all-purpose flour	¼ cup sugar
	½ cup butter

Heat the buttermilk very slightly. Add the yeast. Stir until the yeast is dissolved. Sift the dry ingredients. Cut in butter until mixture resembles cornmeal. Add the buttermilk mixture and beat (in electric beater if possible at low speed) for about 10 minutes. (Dough will be very soft.) Brush melted butter over top of dough (to prevent forming of crust). Cover with waxed paper and refrigerate for 8 hours or overnight. Punch down. Make rolls, put in greased pans. Lightly cover with oiled, waxed paper and let rolls rise in a warm place until double in size, about 2 to 3 hours. Bake for 20 minutes. When rolls begin to brown, brush lightly with melted butter. Makes 2 dozen rolls.

MORNING ROLLS

A pleasant change from the very sweet rolls and coffee cakes.

Preheat oven to 375° *Butter a cookie sheet.*

4 cups sifted all-purpose flour	*Milk*
1 teaspoon baking powder	*½ cup butter or ¼ cup butter*
½ teaspoon salt	*and ¼ cup lard*

Resift the flour with the baking powder and salt. In a large bowl, cut in the shortening with pastry blender or two knives until the mixture is the consistency of coarse cornmeal. Shape a well in the center of the bowl, and gradually add milk until the mixture forms a ball and draws away from the sides of the bowl. Turn out on a lightly floured board.

Roll into a cylinder shape and cut into 8 even portions. Cut off edges of each cylinder to enable dough to rise quickly. Brush top of each cylinder with melted butter or unbeaten egg yolk.

Approximate baking time: 20 minutes. Serve immediately.

A FINE COFFEE CAKE

Preheat oven to 375° *9 x 13-inch pan*

1 egg	*1 cup molasses*
1 cup brown sugar, firmly packed	*1 cup strong coffee*
½ cup soft butter	*4 cups sifted all-purpose flour*
	1 tablespoon baking powder

In electric mixer, at low speed, beat egg lightly. Add sugar and beat until just blended. Add butter and beat again. Combine the molasses and the cold coffee. Mix together thoroughly. Resift the flour with the baking powder. Add the flour and the molasses mixture alternately to the batter, beginning and ending with the flour. Bake in a greased pan for 35 to 40 minutes. Cool on wire cake rack. Cut in squares and serve warm.

SUNDAY BREAKFAST COFFEE CAKE

1894

Preheat oven to 350°   *9 x 13-inch pan*

½ cup butter   ½ teaspoon soda
1 cup sugar   ½ teaspoon salt
3 eggs   1 cup sour cream
2 cups sifted cake flour   1 cup golden raisins
1 teaspoon baking powder   1 teaspoon almond extract

Cream butter; add the sugar gradually and cream until light and fluffy. Add eggs, one at a time, beat well after each addition. Resift the flour with the baking powder, soda and salt. Add the flour alternately with the sour cream (in three portions) beginning and ending with the flour. Stir in the raisins and the flavoring.
Spread in a greased pan and cover with Topping (p. 182). Bake for 30 to 35 minutes. Cool on wire cake rack and cut in squares. Serve warm.

CORN BREAD

Preheat oven to 425°   *9 x 9 x 2-inch pan*

¼ cup sifted all-purpose flour   1 egg
1¼ cups yellow cornmeal   1 cup buttermilk stirred with:
2 tablespoons sugar   ½ teaspoon soda
1 tablespoon baking powder   ¼ cup melted butter
1 teaspoon salt

Resift flour and dry ingredients together. Beat egg until
light and fluffy, add buttermilk and butter. Add all at once
to dry ingredients and beat well with a wire whisk or an egg
beater until smooth and free of lumps. While this preparation is under way, coat the pan with a generous layer of
lard and heat pan in oven. Bake for 20 minutes. Cool
slightly, cut into squares.

SOUTHERN CORN BREAD

Preheat oven to 450°   *Two 9 x 9 x 2-inch pans*

2 cups cornmeal   1 teaspoon soda
2 tablespoons sugar   2 eggs, well beaten
1 teaspoon salt   2 cups buttermilk

Sift the dry ingredients together. Stir the eggs and buttermilk together. Add to the dry ingredients and beat well with

a wire whisk or an egg beater until very smooth and free of lumps. While this preparation is under way, cover the bottom of the two pans with a coating of melted butter or lard. (Bacon fat strained through fine cheesecloth gives an excellent flavor to this type of corn bread.)

Let the pans heat in the oven. Pour the batter into the pans and bake until crisp, about twenty minutes. Cool slightly, cut in squares and serve warm.

This is a good batter for corn sticks. Use heavy corn stick pans heated and buttered.

CORN OYSTERS

Deep-fat fry basket

6 ears fresh corn
1 (10 oz.) package quick-
    frozen corn kernels
1 egg, well beaten
1 to 2 tablespoons milk

1 tablespoon sugar
½ teaspoon salt
Cooking oil
Cube of bread
All-purpose flour (sifted)

Heat the cooking oil until the cube of bread browns immediately when dropped into the hot fat. Cut the fresh corn from the ears. Thaw the frozen kernels. Combine the corn, egg, milk, sugar and salt. Add the flour gradually to form a very stiff batter. The fritters must hold their shape while frying. Drop by spoonfuls into the hot fat and cook until golden brown. Drain on paper toweling and serve hot.

CRUMPETS

1880

Preheat skillet (electric) to   Iron or electric skillet
   340°   4-inch muffin rings

2 cups sifted all-purpose flour   ½ teaspoon salt
1 teaspoon baking powder   2 small eggs, well beaten
1 tablespoon sugar   1 pint lukewarm milk

Resift flour with dry ingredients, add the eggs and mix quickly. Add the milk gradually but keep the batter very stiff. Butter the muffin rings and fill nearly to the top. Bake on one side until a delicate brown. Turn over and bake other side. Cool slightly on wire cake rack and serve warm. These are delicious when split in half, toasted and buttered.

FLANNEL ROLLS

(Today's Popover Recipe)

Preheat oven to 400°   Popover tins

2 eggs, well beaten   2 cups sifted all-purpose flour
1 cup milk   1 extra cup cold milk
¼ teaspoon salt

In large bowl, add the cup of milk and salt to eggs; stir quickly and add all of the flour at once. Add the extra cup of milk and stir with a few swift strokes. Divide evenly in well-buttered Popover tins and bake for 30 minutes, heeding the old admonition: "But never open the oven door until the time is up. If you do the muffins will fall."

PUFFETS

A Nice Breakfast Muffin

1894

Preheat oven to 400°   *Two dozen muffin tins*

2 tablespoons melted butter   1 tablespoon baking powder
2 eggs, well-beaten   ½ teaspoon salt
2 cups light cream   1 tablespoon sugar
3 cups sifted cake flour

Combine butter, eggs and cream. Resift flour with dry ingredients. Add all at once and stir quickly. Batter will be somewhat lumpy. Divide evenly in the buttered muffin tins and bake for 15 to 20 minutes. Let stand on wire cake rack for just a brief minute. Turn out and serve warm.

TEN EGG–WHITE MUFFINS

Gold Cakes, prepared with egg yolks only, were a popular choice for parties when eggs were at the peak of the season. As a result, a bountiful supply of egg whites were available for cakes and delicate muffins.

Preheat oven to 400°   *Four dozen muffin tins*

2½ cups sifted cake flour   10 egg whites
½ teaspoon salt   ½ teaspoon cream of tartar
¼ cup sugar   ½ to ¾ cup milk
1 teaspoon almond extract

Resift flour with salt and sugar. Beat egg whites rapidly until foamy. Add cream of tartar and continue beating until stiff, but not dry. Pour the flour back into the flour sifter, and sift slowly over the egg whites folding over and under until all the white has disappeared. Add the flavoring to the milk, and slowly stir the milk into the mixture. The mixture should be thin enough to pour easily. Fill well-buttered muffin tins ⅔ full and bake for 12 to 14 minutes. Invert on cake rack to cool. Serve at once.

WHOLE WHEAT MUFFINS

1894

Preheat oven to 400°   *Two dozen muffin tins*

1 cup sifted all-purpose flour   *1 egg, well beaten*
1 cup sifted whole wheat flour   *1 cup milk*
2 teaspoons baking powder   *2 tablespoons molasses*
½ teaspoon salt   *2 tablespoons melted butter*

Resift the two cups of flour with the dry ingredients. Combine the egg, milk, and molasses. Add to dry mixture and beat thoroughly. Add the butter and stir in well. Divide evenly into greased muffin tins and bake 15 to 20 minutes. Turn out of tins and serve hot. If left over, these are very good split and toasted.

Pancakes and Waffles

"If you have no eggs for pancakes, supply the place of eggs, by two or three spoonfuls of lively emptings. A spoonful of brandy or New England rum make pancakes light." (1842)

BUTTERMILK PANCAKES

Tender and Delicate

2 eggs
1¼ cups buttermilk
1 cup sifted all-purpose flour
1 teaspoon soda

1 teaspoon baking powder
½ teaspoon salt
¼ cup melted butter

Beat eggs until light, add the buttermilk and stir well. Re-sift the flour with the dry ingredients and add all at once to the liquid. Stir until just barely blended. Do not beat. Stir in the butter. Drop by spoonfuls on a very hot griddle that is lightly greased (unless the griddle is the new type that does not require greasing).

As flour varies greatly, it is advisable to bake a single pancake. If too thick, add a bit more milk. If too thin, add a bit more flour.

CORNMEAL WAFFLES

¼ cup yellow cornmeal
1 pint milk, scalded
2 tablespoons butter
½ cup sifted all-purpose flour

½ teaspoon salt
1 teaspoon baking powder
2 eggs, well beaten
Extra milk if needed

Preheat waffle iron according to directions. Sift the corn-meal over the milk over hot (not boiling) water. Stir and add the butter. Set aside to cool.

Sift the dry ingredients together. Add to the cornmeal mixture; add the eggs and beat well. If too thick to pour easily, add a little cold milk.

INDIAN MEAL PANCAKES

Very Nice, Indeed

Very hot griddle

2 cups buttermilk
1 teaspoon soda — 7⅛ cup yellow cornmeal
2 eggs, well-beaten — ½ teaspoon salt
⅔ cup sifted all-purpose flour — 1 tablespoon sugar

Dissolve the soda in the milk, add the eggs and stir until well blended. Resift the flour with the dry ingredients and stir into the liquid. Let stand about 10 minutes. The batter will be somewhat lumpy. Drop by spoonfuls on lightly buttered griddle. Bake until a delicate brown on one side, turn and bake on other side. Serve hot. Excellent with broiled bacon, ham or sausages.

MAPLE SUGAR PANCAKES

In our grandmothers' cookbooks, there was no whisper of the popular Crepes Suzette of today. But our forebears knew how to make thin pancakes. The delicate little griddle cakes were sprinkled with soft maple sugar, rolled up, sprinkled with maple or powdered sugar and served at once.

THIN PANCAKES

$1\frac{1}{2}$ cups sifted all-purpose
   flour
$\frac{1}{4}$ cup powdered sugar
$\frac{1}{2}$ teaspoon salt

$\frac{1}{4}$ cup melted butter
5 eggs, well beaten
2 tablespoons brandy, good
   quality

Resift flour with sugar and salt. Make a well in the center of the bowl, do not stint on beating the eggs. They must be thoroughly beaten. Combine the butter, eggs and brandy and add to the dry mixture. Beat until smooth. Strain through cheesecloth, cover and refrigerate for several hours. Bake as customary. Spread with jam, or maple sugar or honey or maple butter or honey butter.

MIDLANDS SHORTBREAD

Preheat oven to 375°   *8 x 8 x $1\frac{1}{2}$-inch baking pan*

$\frac{3}{4}$ cup sifted flour
$\frac{1}{4}$ cup cornstarch
$\frac{1}{4}$ teaspoon salt
2 tablespoons confectioner's
   sugar

$\frac{1}{2}$ cup sweet butter: if not
   available, wash salted butter in ice-cold water
$\frac{1}{8}$ teaspoon salt

In large bowl resift flour with dry ingredients. All-purpose flour is preferable to cake flour, but cake flour may be used. Cut butter into flour mixture with pastry blender or two knives until mixture is the consistency of coarse cornmeal. Turn out on lightly floured board. Knead gently and roll out to thickness of $\frac{1}{4}$ to $\frac{1}{2}$ inches. Press down lightly in buttered pan with fingers. Prick the dough with tines of fork. Bake about 20 minutes, until set and a light golden brown. Cool on wire cake rack. Cut while hot into finger length bars, about ½ to ¾-inches wide. Pack in airtight tin. Will keep well for several weeks. Delicious with afternoon coffee.

RICE GRIDDLE CAKES

1894

Very hot griddle

1 pint buttermilk	*2 cups sifted all-purpose flour*
2 egg yolks, well-beaten	*1 teaspoon soda*
1 cup cold cooked rice	*¼ teaspoon salt*
¼ to ½ teaspoon nutmeg	*2 egg whites, stiffly beaten*

Combine milk, egg yolks and rice. Sift the dry ingredients together and add gradually to the liquid. (Batter should be very thick.) Fold in the egg whites and drop the batter by spoonfuls on a lightly buttered griddle. Bake until a delicate brown on one side, turn and bake other side. Good with melted butter, maple syrup or preserves. Excellent with broiled ham, sausages or bacon.

AUNT NELLY'S SALLY LUNNS

1870

This one hundred-year-old receipt reads as follows: "Take a pint of flour, a piece of butter the size of an egg, a saltspoon or more of salt . . ."

20th-Century Recipe

Preheat oven to 375°   *9 x 13-inch pan*

½ cup butter   1½ to 2 cups sifted cake flour
1 cup sugar   1 teaspoon baking powder
3 eggs, well-beaten   ½ teaspoon salt
1 cup buttermilk
½ teaspoon soda dissolved in 1
   tablespoon warm water

Cream butter, add the sugar gradually and beat until light and fluffy. Add the eggs and beat well. Mix the buttermilk and soda water together. Resift the flour with the dry ingredients, and add to mixture alternately with the milk, beginning and ending with the flour. Bake in well-buttered pan for 20 minutes. Cool slightly on cake rack. Cut in squares and serve warm.

Good served when freshly baked, this quick bread is also excellent split in half, toasted and buttered when one or more days old.

SCONES

Preheat and lightly grease an iron skillet or an electric skillet.

2 cups sifted all-purpose flour
¼ teaspoon salt
½ teaspoon baking powder
1 tablespoon sugar

½ cup shortening (butter or vegetable fat)
*1 cup currants, washed and well dried**
Milk

In a large bowl resift the dry ingredients together. Cut in the shortening with a pastry blender or two knives. Add the currants. Shape a well in the center of the bowl, and add the milk gradually to form a stiff dough. The mixture should be just wet enough to form a ball.

Turn out on lightly floured board and roll to thickness of ¼ inch. Cut into rounds and bake until golden brown on one side. Turn and brown on the other. Approximate baking time: 15 to 20 minutes.

* Sprinkle the dried currants with a little flour and shake off the excess flour.

DROP SCONES

Preheat oven to 375°

Butter a cookie sheet.

2 cups sifted all-purpose flour
¼ teaspoon salt
1½ teaspoons baking powder
2 to 4 tablespoons butter

2 tablespoons sugar
1 egg
¾ cup milk (about)

Sift dry ingredients (except sugar) together. Cut in butter

with two knives or a pastry blender. Make a well in center, add sugar and egg. Stir and add milk gradually, just enough to make a stiff batter. Beat thoroughly, until smooth. Drop by spoonfuls on cookie sheet. Bake for 5 to 7 minutes.

SKILLET CORN BREAD

1894

Preheat oven to 375°	*9-inch iron skillet*

2⅔ cups yellow cornmeal	1 tablespoon baking powder
1⅓ cups sifted all-purpose flour	½ teaspoon salt
	2 eggs, well beaten
1 tablespoon sugar	1 pint cold milk

Resift flour with the dry ingredients. Mix the two eggs with 1 cup milk. Add to the dry mixture and mix quickly. Pour into a cold buttered skillet. Carefully pour the remaining cup of cold milk over the top. Bake for 20 to 25 minutes. The cold milk over the top gives a delightful texture to the hot corn bread. Cut in pie shape wedges and serve hot.

SOUR CREAM WAFFLES

If the cream sours before you can use it up, do not throw it away, it makes very delicate waffles.

2 cups sifted all-purpose flour	2 eggs, well beaten
2 tablespoons sugar	1 pint sour cream
¼ teaspoon salt	¼ cup melted butter
1 teaspoon soda	

Preheat waffle iron according to directions. Sift the dry ingredients together. Combine eggs, cream and butter, and add to dry mixture. Beat quickly. It may be necessary to add a little milk to make the batter thin enough to pour easily.

MARGARET'S SPOON BREAD

1894

Preheat oven to 325°   *2-quart baking dish*

1 pint milk	3 egg yolks, well beaten
½ cup yellow cornmeal	3 egg whites, stiffly beaten
1 teaspoon salt	½ teaspoon baking powder

Scald the milk in the upper part of the double boiler, over hot (not boiling) water. Add the cornmeal gradually, stirring constantly. Stir and cook until it is thick and smooth. Let it cool, add the egg yolks, mix thoroughly. Sift the baking powder into the beaten egg whites and fold gently into the cornmeal mixture. Pour into greased baking dish and bake for 40 minutes. Serve hot.

VIRGINIA CORN CAKES

Very hot griddle

2 cups yellow cornmeal	2 eggs, well-beaten
2 cups milk	½ teaspoon salt

Combine all ingredients. Let stand 10 to 15 minutes. Butter griddle lightly and drop the thin batter on the griddle. The batter will be very thin and the cakes thin, crisp and brown. Bake on one side until golden brown, turn and bake other side.

Variation

For a thicker corn cake, decrease the amount of milk to 1 cup. The thinner ones are more delicious, however.

WHOLE WHEAT PANCAKES

2½ cups milk (divided in half)
2 cups whole wheat flour
1 cup sifted all-purpose flour
1 tablespoon sugar

½ teaspoon salt
1½ teaspoons baking powder
2 eggs, well-beaten

Scald 1¼ cups milk, pour over the whole wheat flour, and stir until smooth; add the cold milk and set aside to cool. Sift dry ingredients together and stir into the flour mixture. Add the eggs and beat quickly. Drop by spoonfuls on very hot griddle, lightly greased. These are especially good with ham or bacon.

YORKSHIRE PUDDING

The traditional and classic method of baking Yorkshire pudding was to pour it into the roasting pan in which a rib roast was cooking. But as methods of roasting beef changed, this method was largely abandoned in favor of baking the pudding on the upper rack of the oven while the roast continued to cook on the lower rack.

Method One

Approximately half an hour before the roast is done, remove from oven, let stand in warm place. Pour the hot fat from the roasting pan into a heated baking pan (9 x 9 x 1½). Pour the batter into the hot fat. Place on upper rack. Return the roast beef to its own roasting pan and put it back in oven to finish roasting.

Method Two

Approximately half an hour before the roast is done, remove from oven and pour the batter directly into the hot fat in the roasting pan. Let the roast stand in a warm place, partially covered only. Its internal heat will cook the roast still further, and the meat will be easier to slice if slightly cool.

BATTER FOR YORKSHIRE PUDDING

Recipe I

2 eggs, well beaten	*1 cup sifted all-purpose flour*
1 cup milk	*¼ teaspoon salt*

In large bowl, combine eggs and milk. Add salt and add flour all at once. Beat until smooth, but do not overbeat. Increase oven heat to 425° to bake the pudding.

Recipe II

1 cup sifted all-purpose flour	*½ cup milk and ½ cup water*
¼ teaspoon salt	*mixed together*
1 egg	

In large bowl sift flour and salt together. Shape a well in the center, drop in the egg and beat vigorously. Add the liquid gradually and beat until smooth. Cover and let stand at room temperature for one hour. Pour into pan and increase oven heat to 425°.

Cakes and Cookies

"There is a cake for every man
If he will watch the fire."

A piece of tender, delicate cake, or a slice of rich, delicious cake probably comes closest to being the universal dessert. Its associations range from the time of blowing out the candles on one's birthday cake to cutting the first piece of wedding cake, symbolic of the bride and groom's life together.

A cake has always been the *pièce de résistance* of celebrations, observances and important occasions. Cutting the cake is the highlight of christening parties, wedding parties, birthday parties and anniversaries of every imaginable type.

A wealth of old records describe occasions when a cake, often given a special name, marked the event. One of the earliest descriptions of a Name Cake is that of the Simnel Cake of Elizabethan England, whose name was derived from the Latin word *simila* meaning fine flour.

Another Name Cake was the Mothering Cake. In the days when young girls went out to service, each girl was allowed, according to custom, to go home for the fourth Sunday in Lent, which was known as Mothering Day. For this event she baked a cake to take home to her mother. This Mothering Cake, as it was called, was a heavy, rich cake, filled with raisins and spread with almond paste. A 19th-century cookbook describes it as a rich plum cake, split and spread with the almond mixture.

In early Colonial days, the women carried cakes to church suppers, to barn-raisings, to christenings, and to weddings. Each woman was proud of her own specialty and the old cookbooks frequently named a cake after the friend who gave her the precious receipt. And the story goes that if the cake didn't turn out well for the recipient, she blamed the giver as "leaving out an ingredient."

A number of the receipts in the seventeenth-century cookbooks, such as the following, serve as amusing museum pieces today. No modern housewife would attempt to make:

Course Gingerbread

Take a quart of honey, and set it on the coals and refine it, then take a pennyworth of ginger, as much pepper, as much Licoras; quarter of a pint of Claret wine, or old ale . . .

Almonds were plentiful and were mentioned in many of the old receipts. Among these was Marchpane, the forerunner of modern marzipan, which called for "pounded almonds, pistachio nuts, sugar and flour, with various essences highly ornamented and sometimes gilt."

Many of the cakes were spread with this mixture and it was also served separately as a Comfit, a sweetmeat.

In the sixteenth, seventeenth and eighteenth centuries, the cakes were such elaborate, towering creations, it required a chef de cuisine to prepare, ice and decorate them for their wealthy patrons. Such baking was far beyond the purse of the average man and far beyond the skill of the housewife and her servants.

But by the time the nineteenth century was under way, the homey cookbook writers, who followed the great chefs, began to publish recipes that the housewife and her cook could prepare. And homemade cakes held their own in the family's meals.

The authors made it clearly understood there was to be no nonsense. As one of them wrote, "Good sponge cake is an excellent lunch for an invalid. . . . There is a custom prevalent in many kitchens of using cooking butter; that is, butter that is off-taste. This is poor economy. If you have no other butter for cake, don't make any. . . . And fresh, not store eggs, are an *absolute necessity*.

"The baking of the cake is the most difficult part of the process, on account of the constantly variable condition of the ovens . . . One is obliged to exercise a new judgment every time a cake is baked."

In perusing the accounts in the old books, one is struck anew at the skills, the ingenuity and the enormously long and hard work the women of the previous centuries endured in preparing their appetizing receipts. We should pay a tribute to our forebears by at least recognizing their contribution to our own lives.

Cakes

Hints for Successful Cake-Baking

1. Let the butter, eggs, milk and cream stand at room temperature for about an hour before mixing the cake, except in very hot weather.
2. Egg whites yield greater volume if at room temperature before beating stiffly.
3. A cake is done if it springs back at the touch of a finger instead of leaving a small dent, or if the cake shrinks slightly

from the edge of the pan, or if a cake tester (toothpick or skewer) comes out clean and dry when inserted in center of cake.

4. Angel Food and all types of sponge cakes should hang inverted on a cake rack until cool. Bake in unbuttered tube pans.

5. Cake pans must be greased if liquid shortening, butter, margarine, or lard is used; for cakes rich in raisins, currants, chocolate it is advisable to flour lightly after greasing the pans and shaking off the excess flour, or line the greased pans with wax paper, cut to fit, and grease the wax paper lightly.

6. Cakes with shortening should stand on cake racks for a few minutes, then be turned out and allowed to cool. If wax paper is used, it should be peeled off a few minutes after the cake is baked.

7. Use all level measurements.

8. Always sift flour before measuring. Sometimes there is an appreciable difference between 1 cup of flour, sifted and 1 cup of sifted flour.

Read page 255 on measuring liquids, fats and dry ingredients.

9. Use double-acting baking powder.

ALMOND APPLE CAKE

Preheat oven to 350°   *Baking dish*

6 tart apples
1 cup sugar
1 cup water

Almond Paste Filling
½ cup unsalted butter
½ cup sugar
2 tablespoons cornstarch
1 (8 oz.) tin almond paste

Core, peel and slice apples into quarters. Make a syrup of sugar and water, simmer over low heat for 5 minutes. Simmer the apples until just tender, but holding their shape. Lift from syrup with slotted spoon. Set aside to cool.

Almond Paste Filling

Cream butter; mix sugar and cornstarch together. Cut paste into small pieces. Mix the ingredients together to form a smooth paste. Arrange a layer of apples in the bottom of a baking dish. Spread a layer of the paste over the apples. Cover with another layer of apples and top with the remaining paste. Spoon a few tablespoons of the syrup (in which the apples cooked) over the top. Bake 15 to 20 minutes. Serve warm or cold, with cream or whipped cream flavored with almond extract.

BIRTHDAY CAKE

1850

Preheat oven to 350°   *Three 9-inch round cake layers*

1 cup unsalted butter	3 cups sifted cake flour
2 cups sugar	1½ teaspoons baking powder
Juice one lemon	3 egg whites, stiffly beaten
5 egg yolks	1 teaspoon lemon extract, added
¾ cup milk	to milk
¼ teaspoon salt	

Cream butter; add the sugar gradually and cream until light and fluffy. Stir in the lemon juice. Beat the egg yolks until thick and stir into the batter. Resift the flour with the baking powder and salt three times and add alternately with the milk, beginning and ending with the flour mixture.

Fold in the egg whites. Divide evenly between three buttered pans and bake for 20 to 25 minutes. Cool on cake racks. Spread frosting between layers and on top. Decorate as desired according to the occasion.

BROWNSTONE FRONT CAKE

1894

Preheat oven to 375°	*Two 9-inch round layer pans*

Mixture I
½ cup unsalted butter
1½ cups sugar
2 eggs, well-beaten
⅔ cup milk
2¼ cups sifted cake flour (Set aside ¼ cup)
2 teaspoons baking powder
¼ teaspoon salt
1 teaspoon vanilla extract

Mixture II
Cook together over low heat:
½ cup dark brown sugar
¼ cup milk
2 squares unsweetened chocolate (2 oz.)
When smooth, set aside to cool, and add the ¼ cup flour. Beat well.

Cream butter; add the sugar gradually and cream until light and fluffy. Add the eggs and beat well. Resift the flour with baking powder and salt. Add flour and milk alternately to batter, beginning and ending with the flour. Pour one-half of the batter into a greased pan. To the remaining half of Mixture I, add the Mixture II and blend together thoroughly, but lightly. Pour into a greased pan. Bake the two layers 25 to 30 minutes. Cool on cake rack. Spread chocolate cream filling between layers (p. 241) and sprinkle the top layer lightly with powdered sugar. Eat while fresh. Does not keep well.

CHERRY CAKE

1850

Preheat oven to 350°　　　　　*9-inch tube pan*

1 cup unsalted butter
1 cup 10-X sugar
3 eggs, well-beaten
1 cup sifted cake flour

1 teaspoon double-acting bak-
　ing powder
¼ teaspoon salt
½ to ¾ cup candied cherries,
　cut into bits

Cream butter; add the sugar gradually and beat until light
and fluffy. Add the eggs and beat well. Resift the flour with
baking powder. Add the flour to the batter, beating well
after each addition. Sprinkle the cherries with a little flour,
shake off excess flour and stir cherries into the batter. Bake
in a buttered tube pan for 40 to 50 minutes. Cool on cake
rack. Invert and sprinkle top with powdered sugar. Serve in
thin slices. A tube cake pan cannot be inverted when
buttered. Cake must be allowed to cool before pan is inverted.

CHOCOLATE CAKE

Preheat oven to 350°

*Two 8-inch round or square
layer pans*

2 squares unsweetened choco-
　late (2 oz.)
¼ cup boiling water
½ cup unsalted butter
1½ cups sugar
4 egg yolks, well beaten
2 cups sifted cake flour

2 teaspoons double-acting bak-
　ing power
¼ teaspoon salt
½ cup milk plus
1 teaspoon vanilla extract
4 egg whites, stiffly beaten

Melt the chocolate and water over hot (not boiling) water. Set aside to cool. Cream butter; add the sugar gradually and beat until light and fluffy. Add the egg yolks and stir in quickly. Add the chocolate and stir in well. Resift the flour, baking powder and salt. Add flour and milk alternately, beginning and ending with the flour. Fold in the egg whites gently. Bake in the well-buttered pans, lined with wax paper. When cake is baked, proceed as in the Devil's Food Recipe below.

MONSIEUR GOUFFÉ'S CUSSY CAKES

20th-century adaptation

Preheat oven to 375°   *Two 9 x 13-inch pans*

7 egg whites   *1 cup sifted cake flour*
½ teaspoon cream of tartar   *½ cup cornstarch*
¼ teaspoon salt   *¼ cup melted butter*
1 cup sugar   *¼ cup cold water*
7 egg yolks
1 teaspoon almond or lemon extract

Let egg whites and yolks stand at room temperature for one hour. In electric mixer, at high speed, beat egg whites, cream of tartar and salt until it forms soft peaks. Add the sugar gradually until the mixture is very stiff and shiny. Scrape blades. Set mixture aside. Using same blades, at low speed, beat the yolks and flavoring together until just barely blended.

Resift flour with cornstarch, add to egg yolks, add butter and water and blend all together quickly, or at low speed.

Fold into the egg white mixture, over and under until all pieces of the egg white are absorbed. Line the pans with wax paper and butter both sides of paper. Bake for 20 to 25 minutes. Cool on cake rack for 5 minutes. Turn out, peel off paper and cool. Frost as desired. Excellent for petit-fours.

DAFFODIL CAKE

1880

This cake was always placed in the center of the long picnic table at the annual Sunday School picnic.

Preheat oven to 375°	*9-inch tube pan*
6 egg whites	*6 egg yolks*
½ teaspoon cream of tartar	*⅛ cup very cold water*
½ cup sugar	*1 teaspoon grated lemon rind*
1½ cups sifted cake flour	*and*
1 teaspoon double-acting baking powder	*1 teaspoon lemon juice or*
½ teaspoon salt	*1 teaspoon vanilla or almond extract*
1 cup sugar	

Beat the egg whites with the cream of tartar until soft peaks form. Gradually sprinkle over the onehalf cup sugar and continue beating until mixture is very stiff and shiny. Resift the dry ingredients together three times. Combine the egg yolks, cold water and flavoring. Add to dry ingredients and beat until *just barely* mixed. Pour over the egg white mixture gradually, folding over and over as each addition is made until all white pieces disappear. Scrape bottom and sides of bowl with rubber spatula. Pour into ungreased tube pan. Beginning at center of pan, swirl the spatula (without lifting it) to edge of pan. When cake is baked, invert over cake rack and let hang until cold. Remove from pan and frost with uncooked Lemon Frosting (p. 185) or serve plain or with Lemon Sherbet.

DEVIL'S FOOD CAKE

Preheat oven to 350°   *Two 8-inch round layer pans*

2 squares unsweetened choco-   1½ cups sifted cake flour
    late (2 oz.)   ½ teaspoon soda
½ cup boiling water   ½ teaspoon baking powder
½ cup unsalted butter   ¼ teaspoon salt
1 cup brown sugar, firmly   ½ cup buttermilk
    packed   1 teaspoon vanilla extract
2 eggs, well beaten

Melt chocolate and boiling water together over low heat. Stir until smooth and set aside to cool. Cream butter; add the sugar gradually and beat until light and fluffy. Resift the flour with the dry ingredients. Add the eggs to the butter and sugar mixture. Stir in quickly. Add the flour and milk alternately to the mixture, beginning and ending with the flour. Add the flavoring. Bake in buttered and floured pans (or line the buttered pans with wax paper and butter the paper).

Cake will be very moist. Bake until a toothpick inserted in center of pan comes out clean and dry, or until edges shrink away from sides of pan.

Cool on cake rack for five minutes. Turn out and peel off paper. Do not frost until cold.

DREAM CAKE

1890

Prepare a White Cake Batter (p. 87)
When cool, put the layers together with a Caramel Filling
(p. 179). Cover the top with a white frosting flavored with
rose water (available in drug stores); tint a delicate pale
pink.

ENGLISH CREAM CAKE

Preheat oven to 375°

*A round baking dish or two
8-inch cake layers*

½ cup butter
1 cup sugar
2 eggs, well-beaten
½ cup milk
1½ cups sifted cake flour

2 teaspoons baking powder
¼ teaspoon salt
Resift dry ingredients
1 teaspoon vanilla extract

Cream butter; add the sugar gradually and beat until light
and fluffy. Stir in the eggs; add the milk and flour alternately, beginning and ending with the flour. Add the
flavoring. Divide evenly between the two buttered pans.
Bake for 20 to 25 minutes. Cool on cake rack. Turn out
when cool. Spread the filling between the layers. Press top
layer down lightly. Secure with toothpicks. If a single baking dish is used, split the cake in half and proceed as above.
Sprinkle top with powdered sugar

Filling

1 cup scalded milk	Stir together
3 tablespoons sugar	1 egg, well beaten
1 tablespoon flour	1 teaspoon almond extract
½ teaspoon salt	

Scald the milk in upper part of double boiler. Strain and pour the milk over the dry mixture and return to upper part of double boiler. Cook over hot (not boiling) water until it thickens. Pour a little over the egg and return to heat. Blend and stir for about 1 minute, and add the flavoring. Cool, stirring frequently. Use when cold.

FRENCH CAKE

An author of a nineteenth-century cookbook had this to say: "I have baked this cake for fifteen years and it has never failed to be nice."

Preheat oven to 375°   *Three 8-inch round layer pans*

¾ cup unsalted butter	¼ teaspoon salt
1½ cups sugar	1 cup milk
3 eggs, well-beaten	1 teaspoon rose water
3 cups sifted cake flour	
1 tablespoon double-acting baking powder	

Cream butter; add the sugar gradually and cream until light and fluffy. Add the eggs and beat well. Resift the flour with baking powder and salt. Add rose water to milk and add flour and milk alternately, beginning and ending with the flour. Bake in the well-buttered pans for 20 to 25 minutes. Cool for 5 minutes on cake racks. Turn out. When cold, frost with uncooked icing (p. 185), flavored with 1 teaspoon rose water.

GOLD CAKE

Preheat oven to 375°   *10-inch tube pan*

10 egg yolks
½ cup hot *water*
1 teaspoon almond extract
1 cup granulated sugar

1¾ cup sifted cake flour minus
  1 tablespoon
¼ teaspoon salt
1¼ teaspoons baking powder

Beat yolks until very thick and fluffy. Add the hot water gradually, beating constantly until the mixture is very thick. Add the flavoring. Sift the granulated sugar over the mixture, a tablespoon at a time. Resift the flour with the salt and baking powder three times. Sprinkle over the egg mixture, a little at a time, but fold it over and over quickly. No flour must be visible when the batter is ready to pour into the ungreased pan. Bake until done, about 35 to 40 minutes. Invert on cake rack until completely cold. A Boiled Frosting sprinkled with grated coconut makes a handsome cake.
This is a good cake to make a few days before baking an Angel Food Cake, as unbeaten egg whites, covered and refrigerated, keep better than egg yolks.

HONEY CAKE

The quantities used in this recipe would horrify today's housewife, who usually buys her supply of honey in a 12-ounce jar and her flour in a two-pound package.

But this is how a nineteenth-century notebook reads:

"Take twelve pounds of flour, four pounds of honey, two pounds of sugar and pearlash dissolved in soda."

LEMON SPONGE CAKE

1894 adapted to 20th-century

Preheat oven to 350°   *9-inch tube pan*

6 eggs, beaten until thick   *3 teaspoons cream of tartar*
3 cups sugar   *½ teaspoon salt*
4 cups sifted cake flour   *1 cup very cold water*
1 teaspoon baking soda   *Grated rind one lemon and 1*
     tablespoon lemon juice

Add the sugar to the beaten egg yolks gradually, and beat until the mixture pours from spoon in a ribbon. Resift flour, cream of tartar and salt together three times. Add one-half of flour mixture to egg and sugar mixture, beating constantly. Combine water, soda, lemon rind and juice. Add alternately to batter, beginning and ending with the remaining two cups of flour.

Bake in ungreased tube pan 30 to 40 minutes. Cool on cake rack. Turn out, frost as desired. Or serve plain.

MADEIRA CAKE

1888

Preheat oven to 350°   *9-inch tube pan*

1 cup unsalted butter   ¼ teaspoon salt
1 cup sugar   Grated rind and juice one-half
5 egg yolks   lemon
2½ cups sifted cake flour   5 egg whites, stiffly beaten
1 teaspoon baking powder   If too stiff, add a little milk

Cream butter; add the sugar gradually and cream until
light and fluffy. Beat egg yolks until thick and lemon-
colored. Stir into the mixture and beat until well-blended.
Add salt, rind and juice. Stir in quickly. Resift flour with
baking powder. Add the flour gradually, beating after each
addition. Fold in the egg whites until all the whites are absorbed. Bake in a greased pan 45 to 50 minutes. Cool on
cake rack. Turn out and garnish with wafer-thin strips of
candied citron.

MOLASSES LAYER CAKE

Preheat oven to 350°   *Three 8-inch layer pans*

2½ cups sifted cake flour   1 egg, well beaten
½ teaspoon cloves   ¼ cup very soft butter
½ teaspoon cinnamon   1½ teaspoons soda dissolved in
1 teaspoon salt   ½ cup boiling water
1 cup molasses

Resift flour with cloves, cinnamon and salt. In large bowl gradually add the flour to the molasses, stirring constantly. Add the egg and stir in quickly. Beat in the butter and add the soda water. Stir mixture until well blended. Divide evenly in the greased and floured pans (see Cake Baking Hints, p. 63). Bake about 25 to 30 minutes. Cool on cake rack. Turn out and spread topping between layers, dust top with powdered sugar.

Topping

1 glass of red currant jelly. Turn into bowl and beat with a fork.

MOTHERWOOD CAKE

1880

A dessert suitable for a party

Preheat oven to 350°   *9-inch round pan,*
          2½ or 3 inches deep

Bake a sponge cake and cool on wire rack. When cake is cold, carefully slice off the top of the cake, about one-inch in thickness and wrap in wax paper. Then measure a one-inch wide edge, mark with toothpicks and with a sharp knife, cut center to two-thirds of depth of cake, leaving the one-inch shell intact. (Save the soft center for later use.)

Filling

Soft custard (p. 225)   *½ pint whipping cream*
Red Raspberry jam   *3 to 4 tablespoons sherry wine*

Prepare the custard one day in advance. Flavor with wine. Cover and refrigerate. An hour before serving, cover the cake shell bottom with spoonfuls of jam. Whip the cream, combine with the thick, cold custard and pour over the jam. Replace the top crust of the cake, sprinkle with powdered sugar.

Reserve Cake

Serve reserve or leftover pieces of top layer of Motherwood Cake with ice cream or with a fruit or lemon or orange sauce. Or you may make Snowballs by rolling pieces of the cake in a soft frosting and then in shredded coconut. The children love these.

ORANGE CAKE

1894

Preheat oven to 375°   *9 x 13-inch pan*

4 eggs, lightly beaten   *1 tablespoon baking powder*
2 cups sugar   *Grated rind, pulp and juice of*
½ cup soft butter   *1 orange*
3 cups sifted cake flour

Combine the eggs and sugar, beating the mixture until thick and smooth. Beat in the butter until it is well blended. Sift the flour with the baking powder and add to the mixture alternately with the orange, beginning and ending with the flour. Bake in a greased pan about 30 to 35 minutes. Cool on cake rack, turn out and spread with orange icing (p. 185).

PORCUPINE CAKE

1882

Preheat oven to 350°   *9-inch spring form pan*

½ cup unsalted butter
1 cup sugar
2 egg yolks, unbeaten
¾ to 1 cup milk
2 cups sifted cake flour

1½ teaspoons baking powder
¼ teaspoon salt
1 teaspoon vanilla or almond extract
2 egg whites, stiffly beaten

Cream butter, add the sugar gradually and beat until light and fluffy. Add the egg yolks, one at a time, and beat well after each addition. Resift the flour with the dry ingredients and add to the mixture alternately with the milk, beginning and ending with the flour. Fold in the flavoring and the egg whites. Bake in a buttered spring form pan until done. Cool on cake rack and turn out on deep dessert platter.

Topping

Soft custard (p. 225)   *Blanched almonds*

Wait until the cake is cool. Just before serving pour the cool custard over the top and around the platter. Cover the top and sides thickly with the almonds.

POUND CAKE

In the Complete English CookBook, *the receipt for a Pound Cake is given as follows:*
Take a Pound of Butter, beat it in an Earthen Pan with your Hand one Way . . . beat it all well together for about an Hour with your Hand, or a great wooden spoon.

20th-century

Preheat oven to 325° · *4¼ x 8-inch loaf pan or 9-inch tube pan*

½ *pound unsalted butter*
½ *pound sugar*
5 *egg yolks*
2 *cups sifted cake flour*
1 *teaspoon baking powder*

¼ *teaspoon salt*
5 *egg whites, stiffly beaten*
1 *teaspoon vanilla or almond extract*

Cream butter, add the sugar gradually and beat until light and fluffy. Beat the egg yolks until very thick. Add and beat well. Resift the flour with the baking powder and salt and beat into the mixture. Beat the egg whites until stiff and fold into the batter. Add the flavoring and spread in the greased pan. Bake 45 minutes to one hour. Cool on cake rack.

For a lighter version of this cake, add ½ cup of milk alternately with the flour, or substitute whisky.

Variation: White Fruit Cake

Prepare candied cherries, citron, pineapple, slivered blanched almonds, golden raisins in any combination until you have a full two cups. Sprinkle lightly with flour, shake off the excess flour and fold the mixture into the pound cake batter at the very last.

QUEEN CAKES

Preheat oven to 350°   *Butter individual patty tins.*

½ cup butter or margarine
½ cup sugar
2 eggs, well-beaten
Grated rind 1 lemon

1 cup sifted cake flour
½ teaspoon baking powder
⅛ teaspoon salt

Cream butter until soft. Add sugar and beat until light and fluffy. Add the eggs and beat well. Sift dry ingredients together and add gradually, stirring well after each addition; add grated rind. Fill patty shells ½ full. Bake for 10 minutes. Cool on cake rack, turn out and sprinkle with powdered sugar. Usually served with coffee.

RASPBERRY JAM CAKE

1888

Preheat oven to 375°   *9 x 9-inch pan*

½ cup unsalted butter
⅔ cup sugar
½ cup raspberry jam
¼ cup sour cream
½ teaspoon baking soda dissolved in 1 tablespoon cold water

2 eggs, well beaten
1½ cups sifted cake flour
½ teaspoon nutmeg
¼ teaspoon salt

Cream butter; add the sugar gradually and cream until light and fluffy. Stir in the jam and beat well. Add the cream and the soda water. Stir in quickly. Add the eggs and beat well. Resift the flour with nutmeg and salt. Add gradually, beating well after each addition. Bake in well-greased pan for 25 to 30 minutes.

Cool on cake rack. Turn out and spread top with a thin layer of the jam. This cake is best when served warm.

RUM CAKE

(*Monsieur Gouffé*)

One large sponge cake (p. 85)

When the cake is cool, split in half crosswise. Pour one-half of the syrup (recipe given below) over slowly. There should be enough to moisten the cake, but not to drown it. Replace the top half of the cake and spoon the remaining syrup over the top and sides. Serve at once. It does not keep well. Caution: both the cake and the syrup should be thoroughly cold.

Syrup

1 cup sugar	¼ to ½ cup rum
⅛ teaspoon salt	½ cup candied citron, finely
½ cup water	sliced
	2 tablespoons unsalted butter

Simmer the sugar and water together, stirring constantly until the sugar is dissolved. Do not stir again. Cook for five minutes. In a separate saucepan, warm the rum. Add to the syrup slowly. Taste and add more rum if needed. Add the citron and butter. Remove from the heat and let stand until cool.

SNOW-CAKES

1894

Preheat oven to 375°   *Two dozen muffin tins*

½ cup butter   ½ teaspoon salt
½ cup sugar   1 cup milk
2 cups sifted cake flour   1 teaspoon almond extract
1½ teaspoons baking powder   3 egg whites, stiffly beaten

Cream butter; add the sugar gradually and beat until light
and fluffy. Resift the flour with the dry ingredients and add
alternately with the milk, beginning and ending with the
flour. Add the flavoring. Fold in the egg whites until all the
white is absorbed. Fill buttered muffin tins ⅔ full and bake
for 20 to 25 minutes. Cool on cake rack and frost with
almond flavored frosting (p. 178).

SOFT MOLASSES GINGERBREAD

19th-century

Preheat oven to 375°   *9 x 13-inch pan*

1 cup molasses   ¼ teaspoon cloves
¼ cup unsalted butter   1 egg, well-beaten
½ cup buttermilk   2 cups sifted cake flour
½ teaspoon salt
1 teaspoon each
   soda, ginger, cinnamon

Combine molasses and butter. Simmer over low heat until
it just comes to a boil. Remove from heat, cool and add

milk. Stir dry spices, salt and soda together until blended. Add to mixture. Stir in the egg, add the flour and beat quickly until well blended. Butter the pan, line with wax paper and butter the paper. Bake for 20 to 25 minutes. Cool on cake rack and serve warm.

Variations

1. Stir in 1 cup golden raisins. 2. Serve with Lemon Sauce. 3. Frost with chocolate butter frosting.

SOUR CREAM FUDGE CAKE

Preheat oven to 350°.   *Three 8-inch round layer pans*

⅓ cup butter, softened
½ pint sour cream
2 cups sifted cake flour
1½ cups sugar
1 teaspoon soda
½ teaspoon salt

2 eggs
3 squares unsweetened chocolate (3 oz.)
¼ cup hot water
1 teaspoon vanilla extract

Beat butter and cream together until blended. Resift the flour with the dry ingredients and beat together with the butter mixture for two minutes. Melt chocolate in hot water. Combine the eggs, melted chocolate and flavoring. Beat two minutes longer. Divide evenly in the three pans and bake for 30 to 35 minutes. Cool on cake rack for a few minutes. Turn out on rack and peel off the paper. Cool well before frosting.

This is a handsome cake. As there are three layers, it is advisable to hold layers together by inserting toothpicks around the rim of the two lower layers and on the rim of the upper layer and the middle layer.

For a rich, dark cake, best results are obtained if the pans are lightly buttered, lined with wax paper and the paper lightly oiled or buttered.

SPICY MOLASSES CAKE

Preheat oven to 350°   *9 x 13-inch pan*

¼ cup unsalted butter
½ cup sugar
½ cup molasses
1 egg, well-beaten
Grated rind and juice
   ½ lemon
2 cups sifted cake flour

½ teaspoon ginger
½ teaspoon nutmeg,
1 teaspoon cinnamon,
⅛ teaspoon salt
½ teaspoon soda dissolved in
   ½ cup buttermilk

Cream butter; add the sugar gradually and cream until light and fluffy. Stir in molasses, egg, rind and juice. Beat thoroughly. Resift flour with spices and salt. Add the flour mixture alternately with the buttermilk, beginning and ending with the flour. Bake in the well-greased pan about ½ hour. Cool on wire cake rack. Serve with vanilla sauce (p. 225) or whipped cream.

STALE LOAF CAKE

Our forebears were thrifty women as this receipt tells us: If you have loaf cake slightly injured by time, or by being kept in the cellar, cut off all appearances of mold, wipe with clean cloth, and wet it well with strong brandy and water sweetened with sugar. Let heat strike through it—unless very bad, will restore the sweetness.

THRIFTY SPONGE CAKE

1880

In the twentieth century we are prone to believe we invented the word "diet," but a book written in the nineteenth century states, "Get diet bread and sponge cake into the oven with all possible speed."

Preheat oven to 350°   *9-inch Tube Pan*

3 small eggs   *1½ teaspoons double-acting*
*   or two large eggs*   *   baking powder*
½ cup sugar   *2 tablespoons melted butter*
1 cup sifted cake flour   *1 cup light cream*
½ teaspoon salt

Beat eggs and sugar together until very thick and smooth. Resift flour with baking powder and salt, add to eggs gradually, stirring well after each addition. Add butter and cream; stir in quickly, but do not beat. Bake for 25 to 30 minutes in an unbuttered tube pan. Invert on cake rack until cool. Turn out and sprinkle top with powdered sugar. Test with toothpick or straw before removing from oven.

STRAWBERRY SHORTCAKE

When home-grown strawberries are at their peak, this is the recipe to make. There's never been a better hearty dessert.

Preheat oven to 375°   *Round 9-inch cake pan*

Prepare the recipe for baking powder biscuits (p. 35). Add 1 or 2 tablespoons sugar to flour. Turn out on lightly floured board. Divide in half. Roll each half to fit the cake pan. Butter the bottom of the cake pan generously.

Place one-half of the dough in the pan and cover the top with a light layer of melted butter, or dot with bits of soft butter.

Cover with the other half of the dough, also rolled to fit the cake pan. Bake until golden brown (about 20 minutes). Turn out on bread board and carefully separate the two halves (which will separate easily).

While the biscuit dough is baking, rinse two quarts of fresh berries, hull and crush with sugar. For each quart of berries, about ½ cup of sugar is right. Arrange the lower crust on warm platter, cover lavishly with half of the berries. Place the top crust over berries (underside on top), pour berries over the top and serve at once with cream.

WHISKEY CAKE

Preheat oven to 350°   *Two 9-inch square pans*

½ cup unsalted butter
1 cup brown sugar, firmly packed
4 egg yolks
1¼ cups sifted cake flour
¼ teaspoon salt
¼ teaspoon allspice
½ teaspoon cinnamon

½ teaspoon nutmeg
1 teaspoon baking powder
½ teaspoon soda
¼ cup boiling water
½ pound pitted dates, cut in pieces
¼ cup whiskey

Cream butter; add the sugar gradually and cream until light and fluffy. Add the yolks, one at a time and beat well after each addition. Resift the flour twice with all the dry ingredients (except soda). Add the soda to the boiling water and pour over the dates. Let cool thoroughly, drain and add to the whiskey. Add the flour mixture to the batter; stir in the dates and whiskey. Bake in the buttered pans for 25 to 30 minutes. Let cool on cake rack. Cover each layer with a meringue topping (p. 111) and bake for a few minutes in a 425° oven. Cut into wedges. Serve warm or cold.

Variation

Top the unbaked cake batter with the meringue and bake in the 250° oven. Serve separately or put layers together with sweetened whipped cream. If the cakes are baked with the meringue topping, cake pans with a removable rim are the easiest to use.

DELICATE WHITE CAKE

Preheat oven to 350°   *Two or three round 8-inch layer pans*

½ cup butter
1¼ cups sugar
2 cups sifted cake flour
2 teaspoons baking powder
¼ teaspoon salt
¾ cup milk

1 teaspoon almond extract
5 egg whites, stiffly beaten
(*Be sure butter, milk and eggs are at room temperature for this delicate cake.*)

Cream butter; add the sugar gradually and beat until light and fluffy. Resift the flour with the dry ingredients 2 or 3 times. Add alternately with the milk, beginning and ending with the flour. Add the flavoring to the milk. Fold in the

egg whites very gently until all white pieces are absorbed.
Butter the cake pans, line with wax paper and butter the
paper.
Bake for 20 to 25 minutes, depending on thickness of the
batter. Cool on cake rack. Invert and peel off paper.

Cookies

Hints On Baking Cookies

1. Use a flat cookie sheet, with a shiny surface and a dulled
underside.
2. Sweet butter is the best fat for greasing a cookie sheet.
3. Always place the cookies on a cold baking sheet, or they
will lose their shape.
4. For delicate cookies, use a foil liner which may be peeled
off.
5. If there is not enough cookie dough to fill the last pan,
use a cake pan upside down.
6. Always preheat the oven.
7. Always remove cookies immediately after baking and
cool on wire cake rack.
8. When cookies are cold, store in airtight container. Tin is
usually best.
9. To garnish unbaked cookies with candied fruit, nut
meats etc, etc, dip garnish in a Simple Syrup (p. 224) and
press firmly on cookie.

Three Ways to Handle Cookie Dough

1. Mix dough, drop from teaspoon and bake after mixing.
2. Mix dough, roll out in 2-inch strips and roll strips in

cylinders. Wrap in metal foil and freeze. Cut in slices and bake.

3. Mix dough, cover and refrigerate overnight. Roll in small balls, flatten with fingers and bake.

BACHELOR BUTTONS

1880

Preheat oven to 375°   *Cookie sheet*

¾ cup sugar	*¼ cup firm unsalted butter*
1½ cups sifted cake flour	*1 teaspoon almond extract*
¼ teaspoon salt	*1 egg, well-beaten*

Combine sugar, flour and salt. Cut in butter with two knives. Stir in the egg and flavoring until well blended. Shape into small balls and arrange on a buttered cookie sheet. Bake for 10 to 12 minutes. Remove from pan at once and cool on cake rack. Store in airtight tins.

CHOCOLATE COOKIES

Preheat oven to 400°   *Cookie sheet*

2 squares unsweetened chocolate	*¼ teaspoon salt*
1 cup unsalted butter	*2½ to 3 cups sifted cake flour*
1 cup sugar	*1½ teaspoons baking powder*
2 eggs, well-beaten	*1 teaspoon vanilla extract*

Butter the inside of the top of a small double boiler and melt the chocolate over hot (not boiling) water. The greased utensil will allow the melted chocolate to pour out easily. Cream butter; add the sugar gradually and beat until light and fluffy. Resift the flour with the dry ingredients. Add alternately to the butter mixture with the eggs, beating well after each addition. Add the melted chocolate and flavoring and stir well.

Divide dough in half, shape into rolls, 2-inches in diameter. Wrap in wax paper and refrigerate 24 hours or longer. Cut in slices ½ inch thick. Bake on *unbuttered* sheet for 5 to 8 minutes.

Remove to cake rack at once.

MARGARET'S RICH DATE COOKIES

1898

Preheat oven to 400°	*Cookie sheet*

1 cup unsalted butter	*¼ teaspoon salt*
1 cup sugar	*1 teaspoon soda*
2 eggs, well-beaten	*¼ cup boiling water*
2 cups sifted all-purpose flour	*2 cups dates, finely cut*
1 teaspoon baking powder	*½ cup chopped nut meats*
1 teaspoon allspice	*1 teaspoon vanilla extract*

Cream butter; add the sugar gradually and beat until light and fluffy. Stir in the eggs until well blended. Resift the flour with the dry ingredients (except soda). Dissolve the soda in the water and pour over the cut dates. Let stand for a few minutes.

Add the flour to the batter mixture, beat in thoroughly.
Add the dates, the liquid from the soda water, the nut meats
and the flavoring.

Shape into rolls 2 inches in diameter. Freeze until ready
to bake. Slice in rounds and bake on buttered cookie sheet
for 8 to 10 minutes. Remove to cake rack immediately.
When cold, pack in airtight tins.

Variation: Drop Cookies

Drop the dough by spoonfuls on buttered cookie sheet, far
enough apart so the cookies will not run together.

ROSIE'S GINGER COOKIES

Preheat oven to 400°	*Cookie sheet*

½ cup unsalted butter	or 1½ cups sifted cake flour
¾ cup sugar	1 teaspoon cinnamon
½ cup dark molasses	1 teaspoon nutmeg
1 egg, well-beaten	2 teaspoons ginger
1½ cups sifted all-purpose	1 teaspoon soda
flour (minus 2 tablespoons)	¼ teaspoon salt

Cream butter; add the sugar gradually and cream until light
and fluffy. Add the molasses and egg and beat well. Resift
the flour with the dry ingredients, and stir into the batter
gradually, stirring well after each addition. The batter
should be stiff enough to drop by spoonfuls. It is advisable
to bake a sample cookie. If not stiff enough, add a bit more
flour. If too stiff, add a little molasses or milk.

Butter the cookie sheet well and bake 8 to 10 minutes.

HERMITS

One of the best of the old-fashioned cookies.

Preheat oven to 375°   *Cookie sheet*

½ cup unsalted butter	1 cup golden raisins
½ cup brown sugar	½ teaspoon cinnamon
½ cup white sugar	½ teaspoon nutmeg
(or all white or all brown)	¼ teaspoon cloves
1 egg, well-beaten	¼ teaspoon salt
½ teaspoon soda dissolved in	2-3 cups sifted all-purpose flour
¼ cup milk	

Cream butter, add sugar gradually and beat until light and fluffy. Add egg, soda and milk. Resift flour with salt and spices. Add flour gradually until dough is stiff enough to roll out. Add raisins. Turn out on lightly floured board. Roll out and cut into 2-inch rounds. Bake until golden brown.

For best results, sift flour and add the spices to just two cups. Then if more flour is needed, it may be added gradually, but the spices will be in the first two cups in case more flour is not needed.

HONEY COOKIES

Preheat oven to 375°   *Cookie sheet*

1 cup unsalted butter	3 cups (about) sifted all-
1 cup brown sugar, firmly	purpose flour
packed	2 teaspoons soda
1 egg, well-beaten	1 teaspoon cinnamon
1 cup thick strained honey	½ teaspoon nutmeg
1 cup golden raisins	¼ teaspoon allspice
	¼ teaspoon salt

Cream butter; add the sugar gradually and beat well. Add the egg and then stir until well blended. Set the honey at room temperature. Sprinkle the raisins lightly with a little flour and shake off excess flour. Resift the flour with the dry ingredients. (To be on the safe side, add the spices to the first cup of flour.)

Add the honey and the flour alternately to the batter, beginning and ending with the flour. Stir in the raisins. If in doubt about the amount of flour, bake a sample cookie. If more flour is needed, add a bit. If more liquid is needed, add a little milk.

Butter two cookie sheets and use alternately. Bake 7 to 10 minutes. Remove at once and cool on cake rack.

NUN'S PUFFS

Preheat oven to 225°　　　　　*A wooden board*

4 egg whites　　　　　　　*1 cup sugar (minus 1 table-*
¼ teaspoon cream of tartar　　*spoon)*
⅛ teaspoon salt　　　　　　*1 square unsweetened chocolate,*
1 teaspoon vanilla extract　　　*finely grated*

Let the egg whites stand at room temperature for an hour. Beat rapidly until foamy. Add cream of tartar, salt and flavoring. Continue to beat and as soft peaks form, add the sugar, one teaspoonful at a time. Continue to beat until very stiff and shiny. Gently swirl the grated chocolate into the meringue, using a rubber spatula.

Sprinkle a board with sugar, and shape the Puffs into 3-inch shapes, with a peak at the top. Bake at least one hour. At the end of that time, test one, if the center is still soft, bake 15 minutes longer. Turn off the heat, open the door and let the Puffs remain in open oven until cool. Serve with soft custard sauce, made from the egg yolks.

SHREWSBURY CAKES

The original receipt for this rich cookie was as follows: Rub together one pound of butter, one pound of sugar, one and one half pounds of flour. Add one half cup of cream and the yolk of one egg. Let "rest" for 30 minutes. Roll out and bake.

20th-century

Preheat oven to 375°   *Cookie sheet*

1 cup unsalted butter	*½ teaspoon nutmeg*
1 cup sugar	*2 tablespoons sherry wine*
2 eggs, well-beaten	*2 tablespoons rose water*
2 cups sifted cake flour	

Cream butter until soft, add sugar gradually and beat until light and fluffy. Add eggs and beat well. Resift flour with nutmeg and stir in until well blended. Add liquids and stir in. Let "rest" for one hour in refrigerator. Turn out on lightly floured board. Roll out to ⅛-to ¼-inch thickness. Knead dough gently before rolling out.

Cut into rounds and bake on buttered cookie sheet until golden brown. Cool on wire rack.

SOFT MOLASSES COOKIES

1894

Preheat oven to 375°　　　　*Cookie sheet*

⅔ cup butter and lard
½ cup brown sugar, firmly
　packed
1 egg
½ cup dark molasses
½ cup buttermilk
1½ teaspoons soda, dissolved
　in buttermilk

2 to 2½ cups sifted all-purpose
　flour
1 teaspoon cinnamon
1 teaspoon ginger
¼ teaspoon salt

Combine shortening, sugar, egg and molasses. Beat well. Stir in the milk. Resift one cup of flour with salt and spices. Add to the mixture. Add the remaining flour a little at a time. The cookie dough should be just firm enough to drop from a spoon and hold its shape, but the softer the dough the better. Bake for 8 to 10 minutes on a buttered cookie sheet. Remove from pan at once and let cool on cake rack.

Note: If in doubt about the amount of flour, bake a sample cookie. If more flour is needed, it may then be added.

Variations

1. Stir in ½ cup raisins
2. Frost cookies with Uncooked Lemon Icing (p. 185).

SOUR CREAM DROP COOKIES

Preheat oven to 350°   *Cookie sheet*

½ cup butter
1 cup brown sugar, firmly
　packed
1 egg, well beaten
2 cups sifted cake flour
1 teaspoon baking powder
¼ teaspoon salt

½ teaspoon soda
1 teaspoon nutmeg
½ teaspoon allspice
½ cup sour cream
½ cup golden raisins
½ cup chopped pecan nuts

Cream butter; add the sugar gradually and beat until light and fluffy. Add the egg and stir well. Resift the flour with all the dry ingredients. Sprinkle a little of the flour on the raisins and nuts, shake off excess flour. Add the sour cream and dry ingredients alternately, beginning and ending with the flour. Stir in raisins and nut meats. Bake a sample cookie. If more flour is needed, add a bit. If more liquid is needed, add a spoonful or two of milk.

If time permits, chill dough in refrigerator for an hour. Bake on well-buttered cookie sheet for 10 to 12 minutes. Cool on cake rack.

Pies and Tarts

It seems almost impossible today, but three centuries ago arguments over the nomenclature of pies and tarts raged furiously. Many a friendship of long standing was irrevocably broken by these quarrels.

One of the most notable anecdotes concerns a poverty-stricken young man who foolishly argued with his wealthy aunt on this absurd topic and who was cut out of her will as a consequence. His thesis? "Fruit pies are tarts and apple tart is always called apple pie in polite society."

The most authoritative statements on this matter were written by a Latin scholar who said, "Pie is an abbreviation of patisserie, together with paste, pastry, paté, and patty, a derivation of the Latin 'pistum', past participle of 'pinsere' (to beat together). No matter what the material, if beaten or kneaded together, it is a paste. And pastry is a generic term for all culinary preparations that are served as layers or in cases, opened or closed, of farinaceous paste. Pie is simply an abbreviation. All tarts, therefore, are pies. But all pies are not tarts. The word *Tart* comes from the Latin, *torta*, the participle of *torquere*, to twist. Any paste, twisted or manipulated into a fancy shape is a tart. Uncovered plain pastry is a pie."

The pies were also called "Traps," and when covered

with a top crust were given the title of "Coffin." A small tart was called a "Tartelette" But these learned and scholarly definitions did not bring the subject to an end. Pie was also called a "Crustard," from which, of course, evolved today's "custard."

But before the word custard came to have its present meaning, fruit and milk custard pies were "crustards." So an apple pie became a custard pie, and the variety of apple sold for pies was a costard or a custard apple, and the apple sellers were Costers or Costemongers.

By the turn of the seventeenth century, another term for cooking apples had evolved, the "Coddling" apple. One of the chefs of the period wrote:

"Coddled apples . . . Take green quodlings, (codlings) and quodle them."

From these early definitions and spellings came the receipt for Fruite Foulé.

"Take forty faire codlings green, peel and core, codle, beat, strain with a quarte of cream, mix with sugar."

For a twentieth-century recipe of Fruit Fool, see p. 134.

As may be observed in many of our modern recipes, the fundamental rules as presented in the old cookbooks have not changed to any marked degree. Over and over again, the ingredients are the same, the cookery methods the same, but frequently much less elaborate.

Today's recipes for custard pie are practically identical with the old ones, even though the old receipts used many more eggs per quart of milk than we do today.

A custard is still called by its original name, and when the mixture is poured into an unbaked pie shell and baked, it is a custard pie. In relation to the old, old receipts, a custard pie is relatively a newcomer in the culinary field.

As seen in the records of pies and tarts, a mince pie ranks as the oldest of them all. The original mixture was rich with dried fruits, suet and beef. Now, this, too, has fallen into disfavor and the mincemeat, as we know it today, is a much lighter and more delicate preparation. The basic flavoring, brandy, remains the same.

Many of the favorite admonitions in the eighteenth and nineteenth century cookbooks relating to thriftier receipts and easier methods of food preparation will be recognized in the following excerpts:

"To give a delicious flavor to all sorts of pies, have a bottle of brandy with a wide mouth, into which put your lemon and orange peel . . . Keep the lemon peel in a separate bottle."

Linen Pie

A true predecessor of today's rules for handling a pie crust. When it is desirable that the under crust of a pie be well baked to prevent it from soaking the filling, or when the filling is to be uncooked, a mock filling of old clean linen or cotton rags is laid between the crusts and removed as soon as the crusts are baked."

This is one clearly marked instance where the modern housewife is far better off than were her forebears. One old-fashioned method of baking an empty pie shell is still used however. To prevent the shell from buckling, we still use the old-fashioned method of filling the shell with beans (p. 101).

17th-Century Orange Pudding

In today's nomenclature, this receipt is a Tart. "Take two large Seville oranges, and grate off the rind, as far as they are yellow/ then put your oranges in faire water, and let them boil till they are tender; shift the water three or four times to take out the bitterness; when they are tender, cut them open, and take away the seeds and strings, and beat the other part in a mortar with half a pound of sugar, till 'tis a paste; then put in the yolks of six eggs, three or four tablespoons of thick cream, half a biscuit grated, mix them together, and melt a pound of very good, fresh butter, and stir it well in; when 'tis cold, put a bit of fine puff paste about it and put it in and bake it about three quarters of an hour."

Pies

BAKED PIE SHELLS

19th-Century
One of the most popular varieties of pies are those prepared with a cooked filling which is poured into a baked pie shell. In my grandmother's cookbook, she described her method as follows:" Line a large pie tin with rich paste; be sure and fit the paste well into the curve of the plate and gently smooth from the middle of the plate toward the outer edges; then cut it off even with the edges of the tin. Every bottom crust should be put in this way."

20th-Century
Prepare one-half of the recipe for flaky pie crust, or a variation. Roll very thin. Lightly press into a 9-inch pie shell. With scissors, trim the pastry one inch larger than the rim. Fold over to make a double fold, and pinch together to shape a standing edge. Prick bottom and sides of the crust with tines of fork. Brush lightly with ice water, sprinkle with sugar and bake in preheated oven (400 to 425°). Cool on rack before pouring in filling.

To Prevent Pie Shell from Buckling

Do as the French chefs do: cut a sheet of wax paper one-inch larger than the pie shell. Pour in a quantity of dried peas or beans, or small, clean pebbles. About 5 minutes before the baking is completed, carefully lift out and set aside to use over and over again. Return crust to oven to finish baking.

A FLAKY PIE CRUST

The basic rules for making a tender, flaky pie crust are the same today as they were one hundred years ago. Many of the old-time receipts, such as the following, used lard in place of butter:

2 cups sifted all-purpose flour	*½ cup lard*
1 teaspoon salt	*¼ cup ice water*

Sift the flour and salt together. Cut or chop in the lard with two silver knives or a pastry blender, until the mixture resembles small green peas in size. Add the water very slowly, lifting the dough and blending with a fork until the mixture just holds together. (Too wet a dough will yield a tough crust). If more water is needed, add one teaspoon at a time. Shape the dough between the hands into a ball and wrap in wax paper. Refrigerate for 24 hours and remove one hour before rolling out on board.

A pie shell does not need to be buttered, but buttering yields a nicer brown crust.

Variation

Cut in one half of the shortening with two knives or a pastry blender until the mixture resembles coarse corn meal. Cut

the remaining shortening into small pieces and cut in until
the pieces of the mixture are the size of small green peas. To
make this crust successfully, the shortening must be hard.
Proceed as in recipe for flaky pastry.

A RICH AND TENDER PIE CRUST

2 cups sifted all-purpose flour   ¾ cup shortening, half butter,
½ teaspoon salt   half lard
1 tablespoon sugar   1 egg yolk
¼ teaspoon baking powder   Ice water

Resift the flour with the dry ingredients. Cut the shortening
into the mixture, with a pastry blender or two knives. Chop
and cut until the mixture resembles coarse corn meal. Make
a hole in center of the bowl, drop in the egg yolk and stir.
Add the ice water gradually, using just enough to clear the
dough from the sides of the bowl and to shape into a ball.
Wrap in wax paper and refrigerate for at least an hour, or
overnight.
Turn out on lightly floured board and roll out according
to directions of recipe.
Note: Always brush an unbaked pastry bottom crust with
ice water and sprinkle with sugar before adding a jam or
other soft filling.

ROLLING OUT THE PASTRY

Turn the dough out on a lightly floured board or between
two sheets of wax paper. Roll the pastry as thin as possible
(it takes practice) ⅛ inch thick.

Two-Crust Pie

Divide the pastry in half; roll out one-half and press it lightly into a 9-inch pie tin and trim the pastry at the edge of the rim.

Roll out the remaining half and roll it lightly around the rolling pin. Slip it carefully over the pie filling. Slash three slits in center to allow excess steam to escape. The top crust should fit very loosely over the filling. Trim the top crust with scissors and allow to hang about ½ inch over rim. Press the two rims together. Then fold the top edge under the bottom crust and flute with the fingers to form an edge.

Keeping the Juice From Running Out

The problem of a juicy filling's running over the top and the sides of a pie was just as great in the olden days as it is today, and the old cookbooks offered the following idea.

"A splendid way to fix any juicy pie so it will not run out while baking; tear off a strip of cloth one-half inch wide and long enough to go around your plate or tin. Let half the width lap on your pie, and be sure to lap it good at the ends. Wet the cloth a little and squeeze it out dry."

Today's cookbooks suggest that a pie tape be pressed against the rim for the same purpose.

Hints for Successful Pie Baking

1. Select the correct size of pie shell for quantity of filling.
2. For a flaky, tender crust, handle the dough as little as possible. Too much handling toughens it.
3. The novice has to learn by experience how much shortening to use. Too much shortening and too much handling makes a crumbly crust.
4. The ideal method is to chill the pastry dough overnight.
5. Remove from refrigerator one hour before rolling out the pie crust.

6. Always preheat the oven. A hot oven (425°) is the right temperature to start with.

7. Apple pies need slow cooking after the initial high heat.

8. Always use ice water for the pie dough. Use as little as possible; just enough to form the dough into a ball away from the sides of the bowl.

9. A pie crust may be made at least a week in advance if refrigerated before baking.

AMERICAN APPLE PIE

It is frequently said that our apple pie is our favorite dessert. If that is true, it is because the bottom crust is flaky and tender, the apples cooked until soft, but not mushy, and the seasoning of sugar, flour and spice just right. There are an infinite number of recipes, but basically the familiar apple pie is prepared as follows:

Preheat oven to 425°   *8- or 9-inch pie shell*

Unbaked flaky pie crust,
chilled overnight.

Filling

6 tart cooking apples	1 teaspoon cinnamon
¾ to 1 cup sugar	1 tablespoon flour
¼ teaspoon salt	Soft butter

Wash, core and peel apples. Cut into 8 slices, or if apples are very large, cut in 10 or 12 slices. Arrange in over-lapping slices in pie shell, heaping a little higher in the center. Mix the sugar, salt, cinnamon and flour together and pour into a small shaker with a perforated top. Blending the sugar, salt, spice and flour together helps the cook determine whether she has the flavoring needed. The spice can be in-increased according to tastes.

Sprinkle mixture lightly over each layer of apples. Dot the top layer with bits of soft butter. Cover with the top crust and proceed as in directions for two-crust pie (p. 103).

Bake the pie at 425° for 10 minutes, reduce heat to 350° and continue baking until apples are tender. Slip a thin blade knife through the slit in the top crust to test if apples are done. Cool pie on cake rack.

Variations

1. The old-time cooks had their individual methods for baking a good apple pie: some sprinkled lemon juice over the apples; others sprinkled a tablespoon of flour over the crust before the apples were added. Still others added a tablespoon or two of water, but if the apples are fresh and tart, they do not need extra liquid.

2. Vary the flavoring by using nutmeg and allspice.

3. One-crust pie: omit the top crust.

APPLE DEEP-DISH PIE

Preheat oven to 350°

Deep baking dish (2½ to 3-inches)

Unbaked flaky pie crust (½ of recipe)

6 tart cooking apples

Wash, core, peel and slice the apples. Arrange close together in buttered baking dish. Sprinkle with mixture of:

½ to ¾ cup sugar	½ teaspoon nutmeg or cinna-mon
¼ teaspoon salt	
1 tablespoon flour	¼ teaspoon allspice

Roll out pastry crust. Slash 2-inch cuts in center and cover the dish loosely, allowing the crust ample room to fit over the apples without stretching. Trim the edges, press down with tines of fork dipped in ice water. Bake for 40 to 50 minutes until apples are tender.

Variations

Any fruit may be used as in Fruit Cobblers (p. 162). When berries, such as blueberries and blackberries, are used, mix the berries with the sugar mixture, instead of sprinkling sugar over the fruit.

ONE-CRUST FRESH BERRY PIE

Preheat oven to 400 or 425°   *One-quart oval baking dish*

Unbaked flaky pie crust
  (½ of recipe)
1 quart fresh blueberries, black-
  berries, or sour red cherries,
  pitted

1 cup sugar
2 tablespoons flour
1 to 2 tablespoons cold water
1 tablespoon lemon juice

Rinse berries in cold water, drain dry on paper toweling. Mix sugar and flour together. Butter bottom and sides of baking dish. Cover with layer of berries or cherries. Sprinkle with sugar mixture. Add another layer of fruit and continue until all is used. If fruit is very juicy, reduce quantity of water. Sprinkle water and lemon juice over berries. Cover with crust, trim edges and bake until golden brown, about 20 minutes. Reduce heat to 375° after the first ten minutes. Cool on cake rack. Serve warm or cold.

This is a fine summer dessert and is equally good when baked in individual oval casseroles.

CHERRY PIE

Preheat oven to 400°   *9-inch unbaked pie shell*

Pastry for two-crust pie
1 quart fresh, pitted cherries
¾ to 1 cup sugar, mixed with
the salt and flour.

¼ teaspoon salt
¼ cup all-purpose flour or min-
ute tapioca
1 tablespoon lemon juice

Line the pie shell with the pie crust. Combine all the ingredients and mix well. Fill the shell and dot the top with bits of soft butter. Cover with crust, and slash two or three two-inch slits in top to allow steam to escape. Bake until top crust is golden brown.

Variation: Canned Cherry Pie

1 (No. 2) can pitted sour
cherries, strained
3 tablespoons minute tapioca
1 cup sugar
¼ teaspoon salt

½ teaspoon almond extract
½ cup cherry juice

Combine the dry ingredients, add the cherry juice and let stand for 15 minutes. Add the cherries and bake as above.

GOOSEBERRY PIE

The summer season for fresh gooseberries is short, so try to find a quart while they are still in season, for this delicious pie.

9-inch baked pie shell
1 pint fresh gooseberries
1 cup golden raisins
½ to 1 cup sugar

⅛ teaspoon salt
Grated rind ½ lemon and juice
of same

Rinse the berries in cold water, remove tops and tails. Add the raisins, sugar, salt and lemon. Simmer over low heat until the berries are soft and well cooked. Taste and, if needed, add more sugar. Cool and fill pie shell. Top with a meringue or sweetened whipped cream.

Variation

Prepare a two-crust pie, cool the filling and pour into an unbaked pie shell. Cover with top crust as given in directions (p. 103) and bake until crust is golden brown (400°). Cool on cake rack. This pie is very good served cold.

LEMON MERINGUE PIE

9-inch baked pie shell	*1 pint boiling water*
1 cup sugar	*2 egg yolks*
3 tablespoons cornstarch	*Grated rind 1 lemon*
½ teaspoon salt	*3 tablespoons lemon juice*

Mix sugar, cornstarch and salt together until well blended. Add boiling water and stir rapidly. Cook over hot water until thickened, about 15 minutes. Beat the egg yolks, pour a bit of the hot mixture over the yolks, stir and return to heat to cook 2 to 3 minutes longer, stirring constantly. Remove from heat, cool and pour into pie shell. Cover with meringue (p. 111). Cool on cake rack. Serve cold.

Variation

Substitute scalded milk for the water.

LEMON MERINGUE PIE II

Preheat oven to 425°

9-inch baked pie shell
6 tablespoons cornstarch
4 tablespoons flour
½ teaspoon salt
1 cup sugar
½ cup cold water
1 cup boiling water

1 tablespoon butter
1 teaspoon grated lemon rind
⅓ cup lemon juice
4 egg yolks, slightly beaten
Meringue made with 4 egg
  whites

Mix cornstarch, flour, salt, sugar in top of double boiler. Add cold water. Stir until absolutely smooth. Add boiling water. Cook over direct heat, stirring constantly until mixture boils. Set over hot water, cover, and cook 20 minutes. Add butter, rind, juice, egg yolks. Cook until thick, stirring constantly. Cool. Fill pie shell. Cover with meringue and bake until a delicate brown.

LEMON MERINGUE PIE III

"A soft and creamy filling"

9-inch baked pie shell
3 tablespoons cornstarch
3 tablespoons flour
¼ teaspoon salt
⅞ cup sugar

1½ cups boiling water
Grated rind 1 lemon
½ cup lemon juice
3 egg yolks, slightly beaten

Mix the dry ingredients together thoroughly. Add the water all at once and stir vigorously. Cook over low direct heat until the mixture thickens, stirring constantly. Cover and cook over hot (not boiling) water until thick and smooth (about 20 minutes). Remove from heat, add the rind and lemon juice, stir well. Pour a little of the mixture over the yolks, stir and return to heat, cook until mixture thickens again (about 5 minutes). Cool and pour into baked pie shell. Cover with meringue and bake in slow oven (325°) until the meringue is a delicate golden brown. Cool on cake rack before cutting.

Variation

For a richer filling, add 2 tablespoons butter to the mixture at the last minute. Use 2 more egg yolks.

AN EXCELLENT LEMON PUDDING

1807

"A New System of Cooking . . . By A Lady"

Preheat oven to 350°

5½-inch baked pie shell	Grated lemon rind
4 egg yolks	Juice of 1 lemon
½ cup sugar	¼ cup butter, softened
2 squares loaf sugar, rubbed briskly over lemon rind	

Beat egg yolks with sugar until thick and lemon-colored. Add loaf sugar, dissolved in lemon juice, grated rind and butter. Beat well and pour into pie shell. Bake for 10 minutes or until mixture is "set." Always rinse and dry lemons before using.

LEMON CURD FILLING FOR TART SHELLS

Preheat oven to 375°

One dozen baked patty shells
¼ cup butter, melted
1 cup sugar
Grated rind and juice 1 lemon

2 large eggs, well beaten
⅛ teaspoon salt
Whipped cream topping

Combine butter, sugar, salt, rind and lemon juice. Simmer over low heat until sugar is dissolved. Pour over the eggs gradually and return to heat, stirring constantly until mixture is smooth and thick. Cool and fill patty shells ⅔ full. Top with whipped cream.

MERINGUE TOPPING FOR PIES

Preheat oven to 325°

3 egg whites (room temperature)
⅓ teaspoon cream of tartar

¼ cup sugar plus 1½ teaspoons sugar
⅛ teaspoon salt

Whip egg whites at rapid speed until frothy. Add the cream of tartar and whip until high peaks form but do not whip until dry. Sprinkle in the sugar, one teaspoon at a time, beating rapidly. Add the salt to the sugar.

Pile high on the filling and spread to the very edge of the crust, so it will not shrink away. Bake until the meringue is a delicate golden brown.

Another method of baking a meringue topping is to preheat the oven to 425° and bake the pie for a brief five minutes.

ORANGE PIE

Preheat oven to 400°

Unbaked 9-inch pie shell
1 cup unsalted butter
1½ cups powdered sugar
Grated rind and juice two
    oranges (strain juice)

One wine glass of white wine
2 tablespoons brandy
6 eggs, beaten until thick*

Cream butter, add the sugar gradually and beat until light and fluffy. Add the rind, juice, wine and brandy. Stir well. Add the eggs slowly, stirring constantly. Pour the mixture into the pie shell. Bake for 10 minutes at 400°. Reduce heat to 375° and continue baking until silver knife inserted in center of pie comes out clean and dry, not at all milky. Cool on cake rack. Serve warm or cold.

* Let the shelled eggs stand at room temperature for an hour. Eggs and liquor must be same temp.

ORANGE PIE II

Preheat oven to 350° F

5 eggs, well-beaten
2 cups sugar
Juice and grated rind of 1
    orange

Six 6-inch pie tins
2½ cups sifted cake flour
1½ teaspoons baking powder
¼ teaspoon of salt

Beat eggs and sugar together until thick. Add the orange juice and rind. Resift flour, baking powder and salt and

sift over mixture. Stir quickly and divide batter into the 6
pie tins.
Bake for 20 minutes and cool on wire cake racks. Spread
icing between layers and on top of each pie. Stack three
layers together.

Icing

4 egg whites, unbeaten
1 lb. 10-X sugar
  (more if needed)

Juice and grated rind 1 to 2
  oranges
1 teaspoon almond extract

Add the sugar to orange juice and rind gradually until the
mixture is thick enough to spread smoothly. More sugar
may be needed. Much depends on the size of the eggs and
the amount of the orange juice.
This is a wonderful pie for a party.

MARTHA'S PEACH PIE

Preheat oven to 400°

Unbaked 9-inch pie shell
1 quart peeled and sliced fresh
  peaches

½ cup sugar
1 teaspoon cinnamon
⅛ teaspoon salt

Arrange the sliced peaches in overlapping style. Combine
sugar, cinnamon and salt. Sprinkle lightly over peaches.
A few spoonfuls of lemon juice may be sprinkled over the
peaches. Prepare a lattice pie crust for top, or a whole top.
Bake until golden brown. Reduce heat after the first 5
minutes to 375°. Cool on cake rack.

POT PEACH PIE

Preheat oven to 425°

2-inch deep 9-inch baking
   dish

Pastry for two-crust pie
8 ripe peaches
½ to 1 cup sugar

¼ teaspoon salt
1 tablespoon lemon juice

Line the deep dish with one-half of the crust. Peel and slice
the peaches. Sprinkle with the lemon juice and the sugar.
Cover with the top crust, with two or three slashes in center
to allow excess steam to escape. Bake until crust is golden
brown. Cool slightly, and with a sharp knife, cut the top
crust off carefully.

Lay the top crust in a large, warm platter. Turn the pie
over it, with the bottom crust now on the top. Serve warm
with cream and a sprinkling of nutmeg. It will cut unevenly
and is delicious.

Variation

Use cooking apples instead of peaches.

PEAR PIE

9-inch baked pie shell
6 greenish Bartlett pears
¼ cup sugar
¼ cup water

Juice of 1 lemon
Thin rind of lemon
1–2 inch length candied ginger,
   sliced thin

Peel and slice the pears, set aside in bowl of acidulated water to prevent browning. Prepare a syrup of the sugar, water, lemon rind, juice and ginger. Simmer over low heat, stirring until sugar is dissolved, for about 5 minutes. Strain out the lemon rind and ginger.

Lift pears from water with slotted spoon. Add to syrup and simmer gently until just barely tender. Cool thoroughly and arrange in pie shell, allowing a little of the syrup to drizzle over. Serve cold, topped with whipped cream, garnished with bits of candied ginger.

PEAR PIE II

9-inch baked pie shell
6 whole winter pears

Syrup
1 cup water
½ cup light brown sugar

½ cup light molasses
Rind one-half orange

Select a deep saucepan. Combine the ingredients and simmer over low heat until sugar is dissolved. Peel the pears, leave whole. Gently place the pears in the hot syrup (three at a time) and simmer until just tender. Lift out with slotted spoon and cool. When very cold, arrange in pie shell and garnish with whipped cream.

Variation

Omit the pie shell and serve pears as a compote with whipped cream or a pitcher of cream or soft custard sauce (p. 225).

PINEAPPLE PIE

1890

Preheat oven to 325°

Baked pie shell	*2 cups canned crushed pine-*
½ cup unsalted butter	*apple, well-drained*
1 cup sugar	*5 egg whites, stiffly beaten*
5 egg yolks, well-beaten	*¼ cup sugar (for meringue)*
⅛ teaspoon salt	

Cream butter; add the sugar gradually and cream until light and fluffy. Add the yolks and salt and beat thoroughly. Stir in the pineapple and spread in the pie shell. Cover with meringue of the egg whites and sugar. (See p. 111 for meringue recipe) Bake until meringue is a delicate golden brown. Stand on wire cake rack to cool.

Variation
Omit the meringue and cover the cooled pie with sweetened whipped cream.

QUINCE PIE

1860

Preheat oven to 400°

Baked pie shell	*½ cup sugar with 1 cup water*
2 cups peeled, sliced quinces	*1 to 2 tablespoons lemon juice*
2 cups peeled, sliced tart apples	*½ teaspoon nutmeg*

Over low heat, stew the quinces and apples in a syrup of the sugar and water until just tender, but with the slices unbroken. Lift fruit carefully from stewpan and cool. Add the lemon juice to the syrup and let cook for a minute or two. Arrange the sliced fruit in a baked pie shell, sprinkle with nutmeg and cover with whipped cream. Serve cold.

SUMMER MINCEMEAT

At first glance, the combination of ingredients for this receipt of long ago sounds very odd. But it is a very flavorful substitute for the old-fashioned heavy mincemeat.

Preheat oven to 400° | *One dozen baked tart shells or a 9-inch pie pan*

Pastry for two-crust pie

Roll out pastry to fill bottom of the 9-inch pie pan and the top crust, or roll out the pastry and cut to fit one dozen tart shells, and bake before filling.

Mincemeat

2 eggs, well-beaten
1 cup sugar
1 cup soft, fresh bread crumbs
¼ cup cider vinegar
¼ cup hot water
¼ teaspoon baking soda
¼ teaspoon salt

¼ cup dark molasses
2 cups golden raisins
½ cup melted butter
½ teaspoon each:
cinnamon, cloves
¼ teaspoon nutmeg
2 tablespoons brandy
or sherry

Add the sugar to the eggs and beat until thick and fluffy. Add the bread crumbs, stir in well and let stand for 30 minutes.

Combine vinegar, water, soda and salt. Add the molasses and raisins and let stand for 30 minutes. Strain through clean, damp cheesecloth and set the liquid aside. Add the raisins to the egg, sugar, breadcrumb mixture and stir well. Mix the butter, spices and liquor together and stir into the mixture. Pour into saucepan, simmer over low heat. As it thickens, add the molasses and vinegar liquid slowly, stirring frequently. The final mixture should be very thick, but moist.

If the mixture is to be baked in an unbaked pie shell, use more liquid than if it is to be spooned into baked tart shells. The texture and flavor closely resembles mincemeat. Serve with Hard Sauce (pg. 221).

If the pastry is baked in an unbaked pie shell, preheat oven to 400°. At the end of five minutes, reduce heat to 350° and bake until top crust is golden brown.

Variation

In place of raisins only, currants, candied citron, orange or lemon peel may be combined according to taste, but to measure two cups full.

SWEET POTATO PIE

Preheat oven to 375°   *Two-quart round casserole*

6 sweet potatoes   ¼ cup sugar
6 tart baking apples   ¼ cup melted butter
1 cup white wine

Cook, peel and slice the potatoes. Peel and slice the apples. Butter bottom and sides of casserole. Arrange sliced potatoes and apples in alternate layers in casserole. Mix wine, sugar and butter together. Pour over mixture. Sprinkle top with a little grated nutmeg. Bake in covered casserole as is, or if desired, cover with a rich pastry crust. Bake until apples are tender, about 45 minutes.

Variation

Omit the nutmeg, cover the casserole with pastry crust and bake until apples are tender. A slit in the crust will allow a pointed knife to penetrate the mixture to try for doneness.

WHIPPED CREAM PIE

1882

"*The husband earns, the wife dispenses. Are not her duties as important as his?*"

Baked pie shell
1/2 cup red raspberry jam
1 pint whipping cream, whipped

1/2 cup 10-X sugar
1/4 cup finely chopped candied pineapple and citron
Garnish: glacé cherries

Spread the bottom of the pie shell with the jam. Spread the sweetened cream and fruit mixture over the jam. Garnish the border with the cherries. Combine the filling at the last minute.

Delectable, but should be served as soon as prepared.

Tarts

The oldest flaky pastry was named Bakewell, and as one historian dryly wrote, "Probably because it baked well." Some of the yarns were derived from old customs. Coventry or God Cakes was one. The name came from an English custom observed in Coventry, Warwickshire where children who visited their godparents on New Year's Day received their little gift of God Cakes: flaky little pastries with a rich filling of raisins, currants, citron, and almonds. This custom disappeared, but the little pastry has continued to be prepared.

Very similar to the God Cakes were the Eccles Cakes. These were said to be eaten in observance of an ancient religious festival. The festival has been discontinued, but the receipt has lingered on. Later when the popular Banbury Tart came into being, their ingredients were similar, indeed, to the ingredients in the God Cakes and in the Eccles Cakes.

This was logical, for in all lands and with every generation, housewives were obliged to use whatever materials were at hand, without benefit of refrigerators, freezers, or rapid transportation. And raisins, currants, almonds, honey and citron were well known and used in profusion. But it makes little difference how apocryphal the legends were; our forebears had a sweet tooth and liked sweets as much as we do.

As is true of so many of the old receipts translated into recipes, the Banbury Tart recipe is simpler than its ancestors. The pastry was named after an English town. The tarts were baked, placed in a linen-covered basket and the baker's boy peddled them "hot and fresh Banbury Tarts" on the local streets.

While today's housewife cannot buy them hot and fresh from the baker's boy, she can, in her own ultra modern kitchen make them as hot and fresh as they were three hundred years ago.

APPLE TURNOVERS

Preheat oven to 400°   Cookie sheet

Pastry for two-crust pie	½ teaspoon cinnamon
1 egg yolk	¼ teaspoon nutmeg
2 tablespoons cream	⅛ teaspoon salt
2 cups thick, fresh apple sauce	Soft butter

Prepare the pastry, add the egg yolk and cream. Beat well, form into a ball, wrap and refrigerate: Roll out on lightly floured board. Cut into 4 to 5 inch-rounds. Mix the apple sauce with spices, salt and 1 teaspoon soft butter to each spoonful. Place the mixture on one-half of the round, fold over other half. Press edges together with fork dipped in ice water. Bake on well-buttered cookie sheet until golden brown. Cool on cake rack. Sprinkle with powdered sugar and serve warm.

BAKEWELL TARTS

Bakewell tarts were very popular sweets, and the old cookbooks contained many versions of the receipt. The following are the most representative of the many encountered in browsing through the old books.

I

Preheat oven to 400°   *A shallow oval baking dish*

Flaky pie crust   *¼ cup sugar*
Red raspberry jam   *Grated rind 1 lemon*
4 egg yolks   *¼ cup lemon juice*

Divide pastry in half, line bottom and sides with thinly rolled out crust. Prick bottom and sides with fork, brush lightly with ice water and sprinkle with sugar. Spread with jam or spread the jam over the filling. Beat egg yolks until thick. Add sugar, lemon rind and juice. Pour over the jam and cover with top crust. Trim edges and press down with fork dipped in ice water. Cut 2 or 3 slits in crust to allow excess steam to escape. Bake at 400° for 5 minutes. Reduce heat to 350 and continue baking until crust is golden brown. Cool on wire rack. Serve warm.

II

Preheat oven to 400°   *5-inch oval baking dish or un-*
                                          baked patty shells

Flaky pie crust   *⅛ teaspoon salt*
½ cup unsalted butter   *Red raspberry jam*
1 cup sugar   *½ cup soft, fresh bread crumbs*
2 eggs, well-beaten   *1 teaspoon vanilla extract*

Line the bottom and sides of the baking dish with crust. Prick bottom and sides with fork. Brush with ice water, sprinkle with sugar and spread with jam. Melt the butter, add the remaining ingredients and stir well. Pour into the lined dish. Roll out a top crust, make cuts in center to allow steam to escape.

Bake for 5 minutes, reduce the heat to 350° and continue baking until top crust is golden brown. Cool on cake rack. Serve warm with cream. May also be worked into unbaked patty shells.

BANBURY TARTS

20th-century

There are many versions of this recipe, but this one, many think, is the best.

Preheat oven to 400°

1 dozen baked tart shells
1 cup sugar
½ cup raisins
½ cup currants
1 soda cracker, rolled fine

1 egg, well-beaten
Grated rind and juice of one lemon
2 or more tablespoons candied lemon peel, sliced very thin

Combine all ingredients, and cook over low heat until it thickens. Cool and fill the baked shells.

Variations
1. Substitute all raisins for currants.
2. For a richer pastry, add 2 tablespoons butter. Taste when the mixture is cool, and add more lemon juice if needed. The soda cracker is the traditional one to use.

GOD CAKES
(Coventry Cakes)

17th-century

Preheat oven to 400°　　　　　*Cookie sheet*

Flaky pie crust
1 cup unsalted butter
1 cup dark brown sugar, firmly
　packed
1 cup finely sliced candied lemon
　and/or orange peel

$1\frac{1}{2}$ cups golden raisins
$1\frac{1}{2}$ cups currants
2 teaspoons allspice
1 teaspoon cinnamon
1 teaspoon nutmeg

Cream butter; add the sugar gradually and cream until light and fluffy. Add remaining ingredients and simmer over low heat until thick and well-blended. Stir occasionally. Cool thoroughly. Roll pastry out and cut into four-inch squares. Place a spoonful of the filling in the center of the square. Fold the corners over to form a triangle. Press edges together with a fork dipped in ice water. Arrange on buttered cookie sheet and bake 10 to 15 minutes. Cool on wire cake rack. Pack in airtight tins.

RICHMOND MAIDS–OF–HONOUR

Another delicacy which has survived the test of time is Richmond Maids-Of-Honour Tart. There are a number of legends, the first of which is attributed to Henry VIII. As the story runs, the King was strolling in the Richmond Gardens one day and seeing the maids of honour enjoying the little pastries, he promptly took one and dubbed it Richmond Maids-Of-Honour.

Another tale, which seems much more credible, concerns a local baker who was so impressed by the Royal Family he created the pastries and gave them their name. However, the legend continues to the throne of Queen Elizabeth I. It was said the Queen named them after her own Ladies-In-Waiting.

Finally, after another century, the yarn comes to rest with King George II, who was said to have named the tartelettes after Queen Anne's Ladies-In-Waiting.

I

(Henry VIII)

This receipt, which has been faithfully preserved century after century, is very delicate and good. According to modern nomenclature, these pastries resemble a baked lemon custard, thickened with bread crumbs.

Since the proportions of ingredients in old cook books differ considerably from today's level measurements, the ingredients are updated for accuracy.

Preheat oven to 400°

Flaky pie crust
One dozen unbaked tart shells

1¼ cups milk, scalded and strained	*½ cup sugar*
	½ cup soft butter
⅛ teaspoon salt	*2 eggs, well-beaten*
1 cup soft, fresh bread crumbs	*Grated rind and juice 1 lemon*
	½ cup blanched sliced almonds

Pour milk over salt, bread crumbs, sugar and butter. Stir and let stand 1 hour. Line the shells with pastry. Prick bottom and sides with fork. Brush lightly with ice water and sprinkle with sugar. Beat the eggs and lemon juice (and rind) together. Add to the crumb mixture, stir in almonds. Fill the shells ⅔ full. Bake at 400° for 5 minutes. Reduce heat to 350° and continue baking until silver knife inserted in center of tart comes out dry and not milky. Cool on wire rack. Serve warm.

II

(Elizabeth I)

Preheat oven to 400°

Flaky pie crust
One dozen unbaked tart shells
1 cup powdered sugar
1 cup ground almonds (or
*   8 oz. can almond paste),*
*   cut in bits*
1 tablespoon flour

¼ teaspoon salt
1 egg, well-beaten
2 tablespoons whipping cream
1 tablespoon rose water
*   (available at drug stores)*

Line the tart shells with the pastry dough. Prick bottom and sides with fork. Sprinkle lightly with granulated sugar. Combine all ingredients and beat until well blended. Fill shells ⅔ full. Bake for 5 minutes at 400°. Reduce heat to 350° and bake until mixture is firm to touch. Cool on cake rack. Top with whipped cream. Serve warm or cold.

Cold Desserts, Ice Creams, and Puddings

BAKED APPLES

*"A little sugar in anything savory.
A little salt in anything sweet."*

6 tart cooking apples
2 cups water
2 cups sugar
¼ teaspoon salt

6 tablespoons golden raisins
6 tablespoons brown sugar
6 tablespoons soft butter

Core the apples, peel a deep ring around the top, about ⅓ down the apples. Make a syrup of the sugar, water and salt and drop the apples into the simmering syrup. Do not crowd the apples. If necessary cook three at a time. When the apples are barely soft, lift from the syrup and arrange in baking dish.

Preheat the oven to 350°. Fill the cavity of each apple with the raisins and brown sugar. Brush the top of each apple with the soft butter and sprinkle with a little more brown sugar. Bake until the apples are tender, but hold their shape. Let stand until cool and refrigerate until very cold. Serve with cream. The apples must be cooking variety. Eating apples are not satisfactory.

BIRD'S NEST PUDDING

This is a very special and spectacular pudding, created to serve for dessert on Easter Sunday. It is well worth the time and trouble it takes to prepare. It is a four-part dessert, made in advance and put together at the last minute: part 1, Orange Peel Nests (make four days ahead of time; part 2, Blanc Mange "Eggs" both brown and white (make one day ahead of time); part 3, Orange Jello Base (make one day ahead of time); and part 4, Soft Custard (make one day ahead of time).

Part 1, Orange Peel Nests

6 navel oranges
2 cups or more of Simple Syrup (pg. 224)

Carefully cut the orange peel in quarters from top to bottom of oranges. Remove the peel, cover with cold water and let stand overnight. In the morning, drain the peel and cut it into thin Julienne strips. Bring the syrup to boiling point, add the strips, stir until all are well-coated and let stand 24 hours.

On the following morning, drain the peel, set aside, and bring the syrup to the boiling point, reduce the heat and simmer until it spins a thread. Add the rind. Let stand for 24 hours. Repeat this process for three successive days, or until the rind is easily pierced with a toothpick or a skewer. Drain the peel, place on a heat-proof platter and let it dry out in an oven set at 300°. Line six custard cups with heavy-duty metal foil, arrange the strips of peel across the bottom and up the sides in criss-cross fashion. At serving time, remove foil.

Part 2, Blanc Mange "Eggs"

(White)
½ cup cold water
1½ tablespoons unflavored
   gelatin
1¾ cups of milk, scalded
   and strained through
   cheesecloth

¼ teaspoon salt
½ cup sugar
1 teaspoon vanilla extract

Sprinkle the gelatin over cold water, stir and let stand to soften. Combine milk, salt, sugar and flavoring. Stir until sugar is dissolved and pour over gelatin. Stir well and let it cool (but not set).

(Brown)
Prepare the white blanc mange and add 1 square of unsweetened, melted chocolate to the hot milk mixture.

Part 3, Orange Jello Base

2 packages orange-flavored Jello

Prepare according to directions on package. Pour into large oblong dish. Refrigerate for 24 hours. At serving time, break up jello with fork, and spread on the serving platter as a base for the "Nests."

How To Prepare Egg Shells
Gently tap the small end of each of 12 eggs with the back of a teaspoon. Carefully pick off the broken bits of shell. Hold the egg upside down and gently twirl over a bowl. The egg will flow out easily. Reserve the yolks and whites of six eggs for the Soft Custard. (The remaining six can be covered and

129

refrigerated for other baking needs.) Rinse the shell in a dribble of water. Stand the empty shells upright in the egg carton.

Part 4, Soft Custard

(See recipe on pg. 225) Use the six eggs to one quart of milk.

How To Fill Shells

When the vanilla and chocolate blanc mange is cool, but not "set," hold a tiny funnel over each egg shell and pour in the exact amount of filling. An easy method is to fill one egg shell with cold water, measure the amount, then measure the amount of blanc mange accordingly.

Place the shells in the refrigerator for 24 hours. Just before dinner, gently tap each shell with the back of a spoon and pick off the shell. It will come off easily. Place an "Egg" in each nest, and add the extra ones as a garnish around the platter.

Serve with a sauceboat of very cold soft custard.

BURN'T ORANGES

Let us go down to Vanessa's and eat Burn't Oranges.
DEAN SWIFT

Preheat oven to 375°	*Heat-proof baking dish (buttered)*
4 large navel oranges	¼ cup unsalted butter
4 tablespoons sugar	2 tablespoons sugar
4 oz. Irish whiskey	½ cup orange juice

Rinse oranges in cold water, wipe dry and peel. Cut peel into thin Julienne strips. Sprinkle with the four tablespoons sugar and pour whiskey (2 oz.) over. Stir well, cover and let stand one hour. Cut the oranges in half and arrange in the baking dish. Cut the butter into bits and dot pieces over oranges. Sprinkle the two tablespoons of sugar over the oranges and bake for 10 minutes. The sugar will caramelize (burn't) in the bottom of the dish.

While the oranges are cooking, prepare a syrup: One-half cup of orange juice, one quarter cup sugar. Simmer over very low heat until sugar is dissolved. Add the Julienne mixture, stir well and simmer five more minutes. Set aside to keep warm.

Remove oranges from oven, remove to a warm heat-proof platter, or a chafing dish. Pour the Julienne syrup mixture into the empty baking dish and scrape the caramelized bits of sugar from the bottom. Pour over the oranges.

While these steps are being followed, warm the additional two ounces of whiskey in a very small saucepan. Ignite and pour over oranges, spoon up the flaming liquid and continue to pour over the oranges until the flame dies down. Serve at once with cream or ice cream.

Note: Liquor will not ignite unless it and the other liquids are hot.

LEILA'S CHOCOLATE PUDDING

1 quart milk, scalded (minus ¼ cup)
6 tablespoons cornstarch
¾ to 1 cup sugar
¼ teaspoon salt

4 squares unsweetened chocolate, melted
2 teaspoons vanilla extract
2 stiffly beaten egg whites

Scald the milk in upper part of double boiler. Stir the dry ingredients together. Add ¼ cup cold milk and stir until smooth. Pour a portion of the hot milk over and stir well. Return to heat and stir constantly until it thickens. Cover and continue to cook for 15 to 20 minutes (to cook starch thoroughly). Stir occasionally. Add the chocolate and the flavoring. Stir well and cool. (For a more delicate pudding, fold in the egg whites). Pour the cooled pudding into dessert glasses and serve with cream or a custard sauce.

CHOCOLATE-RUM DESSERT

4 squares unsweetened chocolate	1 envelope unflavored gelatin
1 cup sugar	¼ cup cold water
⅛ teaspoon salt	2 tablespoons light Bacardi rum
½ cup milk	½ pint heavy cream
3 eggs, separated	1 to 2 tablespoons 10-X sygar

Combine chocolate, sugar, salt and milk in upper part of double boiler. Simmer over hot (not boiling) water until chocolate is melted. Stir occasionally. Beat egg yolks until thick. Sprinkle gelatin over cold water, stir and let stand until softened. Add egg yolks to gelatin, stir and slowly add the hot chocolate mixture, a little at a time, stirring constantly.

Return to heat (over hot water) and continue to stir until mixture is smooth and free from lumps. Strain through wet cheesecloth. Fold in rum and stiffly-beaten egg whites. Pour into parfait glasses. Chill for several hours. Garnish with whipped cream, sweetened with 10-X sugar.

COLD FRUIT SOUFFLÉS

(Apricots, Peaches, Pears)

6 egg yolks

½ cup sugar

¼ cup hot Simple Syrup

⅛ teaspoon salt

2 cups puréed fruit*

2 tablespoons gelatin

½ cup cold water

1 pint whipping cream (divided in half)

* Dried apricots are best for this dessert. Canned peaches and canned pears may also be used.

Simple Syrup

Use equal parts of sugar and water. Simmer over low heat for five minutes, stir until sugar is dissolved. Cool and refrigerate. Use as needed.

Soufflé

Beat egg yolks until thick, add the sugar gradually and continue beating until the mixture falls from the spoon like a ribbon. Add the hot syrup very slowly, beating all the time. Add the salt and the puréed fruit. Sprinkle the gelatin over the cold water. Melt over hot water until dissolved. Whip half the cream to a stiff froth, and slowly add the *cooled* gelatin. Fold the mixture into the puréed fruit mixture. Pour into a large dessert bowl, and just before serving cover with the remaining half of the whipped cream. Garnish with glacé cherries, or candied violets or pieces of the fruit.

GOOSEBERRY FOOL

A Fool is a purée of any fruit or berry, cooked in very little water, and pressed through a fine sieve. Its name was derived from the French word "foule" meaning to press or tread (grapes). The cooked pulp is sweetened and chilled. At the last minute, whipped cream is folded into the mixture and the lovely creation served in tall glasses.

1 quart fresh gooseberries	*½ cup sugar*
1 cup water	*½ pint whipping cream*

Rinse berries in cold water, remove any bits of twigs or leaves. Head and tail the berries. Add the water and simmer over low heat until the berries are very soft and the skins burst open. Press through a fine sieve and add the sugar, stirring until the sugar is dissolved. Set aside to cool. At serving time, whip and fold in the cream. Pile high in parfait glasses. If fresh berries are not available, canned or frozen berries may be used. Omit the sugar and water, replace with the fruit syrup.

LEMON CREAMS

In the parts of the country where milk and cream were plentiful in the nineteenth century, the desserts took on a lavishness which is far removed from today's dependence on cream substitutes and desserts low in calories. Modern housewives prepare a Lemon Cream that has little resemblance to this receipt which is delicious.

19th-century
Let one quart of thick cream simmer, sweeten with sugar, cool and add juice one lemon, zest of lemon, prepare early in the morning.

20th-century

1 envelope unflavored gelatin	*Grated rind 1 lemon*
¼ cup cold water	*Juice 2 lemons*
4 egg yolks	*4 egg whites, stiffly beaten*
¾ cup sugar	*½ pint whipping cream,*
⅛ teaspoon salt	*whipped*

Sprinkle gelatin over cold water to soften. Place over hot water and stir until dissolved. Cool slightly. Beat egg yolks until thick, add the sugar and beat until the mixture falls from the spoon in a ribbon. Simmer over hot (not boiling) water until the mixture clings to the spoon. Stir constantly. Add the gelatin, lemon rind and juice. Cool, stirring occasionally, but do not allow to thicken too much. Fold in the egg whites and the cream. Pile high in a dessert dish.

19th-CENTURY LEMON CUSTARD

8 egg yolks	*1 pint boiling water*
Grated rind 2 lemons	*1 wine glass white wine*
Juice 2 lemons	*½ wine glass brandy*
1 cup sugar mixed with 1 tea-	
spoon flour	

Beat egg yolks until thick. Add rind, juice, sugar, and flour. Add the water slowly and simmer over hot (not boiling) water until mixture thickens. Warm the wine and brandy in small saucepan, add to mixture slowly, stirring constantly. Cool and pour into parfait glasses. Refrigerate for several hours. Serve with whipped cream topping.

The leftover egg whites may be used for an Angel Food Cake.

MACAROON SWEETS

17th-century

This receipt is said to be the oldest dessert in England. It appears in some old notebooks written by the wives of the early settlers.

1 to 2 dozen almond macaroons	*¾ cup sugar*
1 pint whipping cream	*Juice of 2 lemons*
Thin peel of two lemons	

Line a shallow glass dessert dish with the macaroons. Combine the cream and the lemon peel; simmer over low heat, stirring constantly until the cream is scalding hot. Do not allow it to come to a boil. Strain out the lemon peel. Let the cream stand until a drop on the wrist is lukewarm.

Combine the sugar and the lemon juice, let stand until the sugar is completely dissolved. Add to the cream, a few drops at a time, stirring constantly. This must be done very slowly, otherwise the cream will curdle. Pour the mixture over the macaroons. Cover and refrigerate for 24 hours. Garnish with glacé cherries.

RICE PUDDINGS

16th-Century Receipt

Take a half pound of rice, and steep it in new milk a whole night, and in the morning drain it, and let the milk drop away, and take a quart of the best, sweetest and thickest Cream, and put the Rice into it and boyl it a little; then set it to cool for an hour or two, and after put in the Yolks of half a dozen Eggs, a little Pepper, Cloves, Mace, Currants, Dates, Sugar and Salt, and having mixt them well together, put in great store of beef suet well beaten, and small shred, and to put it into the forms and boyl them as before shewed and serve them after a day old.

18th-Century Receipt

Take the best and sweetest Cream and boyl it with good store of Sugar and Cinnamon, & a little Rose water, then take it from the fire, and put it into clean pick'd Rice, but not so much as to make it thick, then yolks of six Eggs, two Whites, Currants, Cinnamon Sugar, Rose water and salt, then put it into a pot and so bake it, and serve it in the pot it is baken in; triming the top with Sugar.

SNOWBALLS

18th-century

6 large, firm navel oranges
2 egg whites, stiffly beaten
⅛ teaspoon salt

1 cup 10-X sugar
1 cup shredded coconut

137

Peel oranges carefully, removing all of the white pith. Let stand on rack to drain. Preheat oven to 250°. Add the salt to egg whites and beat until stiff; add the sugar gradually and continue beating until mixture is very stiff and shiny. Coat each orange with the mixture and arrange on trivet on a heavy wooden board. Bake in oven until the meringue is a delicate golden brown. Sprinkle with the coconut and serve at once. Use a dessert fork and knive to serve each guest.

MONSIEUR GOUFFÉ'S SNOW EGGS

1868

1 quart milk	*6 egg whites*
¼ cup sugar	*½ cup sugar*
Rind of 1 lemon	

Bring milk to full, rolling boil with sugar and lemon rind. Beat the egg whites until stiff; add the sugar gradually and continue beating until this meringue is very stiff and shiny. (If using an electric mixer, turn to top speed.)
Dip a tablespoon in cold water, scoop up a spoonful of the meringue, shape it to egg shape, drop several of these spoonfuls on top of the milk, but not close together. Choose a wide top saucepan.

Reduce heat to simmer, and carefully lift the Snow Eggs from the milk. The eggs need to simmer about 4 minutes. Arrange in mound and serve with soft custard sauce prepared from the left over egg yolks.

SYLLABUB

18th-century

1 lump sugar rubbed on a lemon rind	*Sugar to taste*
Juice 1 lemon	*Red wine*
1 pint whipping cream	*White wine*

Let sugar and juice stand until sugar is dissolved. Fill one half the number of wine glasses with red wine and one half with white wine. Now whisk cream, lemon juice and sugar together until frothy. Whisk off froth and place on the glasses of wine until all is used.

SYLLABUB II

20th-century

1 (12 oz.) bottle white wine	*1 pint whipping cream*
2 tablespoons lemon juice	*1 teaspoon almond or lemon ex-*
1 cup sugar	*tract*

Chill wine in refrigerator. Add the lemon juice and sugar. Stir until the sugar is dissolved. Cover and refrigerate for several hours.

Chill a large bowl, a wire whisk or a rotary beater. Pour in the cream and chill for one hour. Slowly add the wine mixture, stirring constantly. Beat vigorously until the mixture begins to thicken. As it thickens, scoop up the mixture by spoonfuls and pour into parfait glasses. Continue to beat and scoop up until all is used. Cover the glasses and refrigerate. A small amount of the liquid will settle in the bottom of the glasses.

This is delicious as is, but a spoonful of strawberry preserves adds a delightful flavor.

ENGLISH TRIFLE

Our English friends tell us there are as many recipes for trifle as there are Englishwomen. The following recipe is a gift from Jean W., from Warwickshire.

1 package of lady fingers
1 cup cream sherry
1 package sherry wine gelatin dessert or any red gelatin
1 cup heavy whipping cream

1 package whole blanched almonds, glace cherries, silver decors and such for decoration

For each of the 3 layers of blanc mange:

2½ cups milk
4 level tablespoons cornstarch

4 tablespoons sugar

Into your prettiest glass bowl (3-pint capacity), break lady fingers in half and pour the sherry over them. Prepare the wine gelatin dessert according to directions and, while it is still warm, pour over the lady fingers. Place bowl in refrigerator to set. It can remain in refrigerator for a day or two until you are ready to prepare the blanc mange layers, as follows:

First layer: put sugar and cornstarch in medium-sized mixing bowl. Blend smoothly a little of the milk. Pour remainder of the 2½ cups of milk into saucepan and bring *almost* to a boil (be sure it does not boil), then pour over cornstarch and sugar, stirring constantly. Return mix to saucepan and stir on low heat until it thickens and is cooked (about 2 minutes).

Remove saucepan from heat, add about ¾ tablespoon of one of your preferred flavorings—say, orange extract—and enough food coloring to produce appropriate pastel shade. Pour over the first layer in the bowl (lady fingers and wine and wine gelatin) and return to refrigerator to cool until set.

Second layer of blanc mange: repeat the above directions, but change flavoring and coloring. For example, this layer may be coffee-flavored by adding one tablespoon coffee-flavored syrup or dissolved instant coffee to the blanc mange. Place in refrigerator to cool until set.

Third layer: prepare as above, again with a different flavor—strawberry for example, by adding one tablespoon strawberry jelly to the blanc mange, together with one tablespoon food coloring. Again, place bowl in refrigerator to cool until set.

Finally, whip cream until stiff and spread smoothly over top of the layers. Decorate with blanched almonds, glace cherries and silver ball decors. (Fresh strawberries and other fruit can be used as well, or a topping of shaved chocolate.) When serving, scoop with a large spoon from bottom of bowl so that each portion will include the vari-colored layers.

"WHAT'S A DASHER?"

A little girl was poking around on the lawn where a farm auction was in progress. She came upon the dismembered parts of an old White Mountain Ice Cream Freezer. She held up the warped and rusted dasher. "What's this?" she wanted to know. Hearing the explanation, she couldn't believe that once upon a time, people actually made ice cream at home.

But in her grandmother's day, an ice cream freezer was as essential a part of kitchen equipment as today's back yard barbecue grill is to modern households. But the ice cream freezer hadn't always been a well-established piece of kitchen equipment. For while frozen water ices and creams had long been familiar in the European capitals, the United States first tasted the frozen confection in Thomas Jefferson's day.

When Mr. Jefferson, served his country as Minister to France in 1784 he was served his first dish of ice cream. History does not record what diplomatic wiles he employed to coax the recipe from a French chef, but coax it he did. And many an experiment must have been carried out to reproduce the unknown recipe upon Mr. Jefferson's return home.

Our forebears took the new dessert to their hearts. The early cookbooks soon bloomed with many a receipt, accompanied by the most minute directions for mixing the ingredients and preparing the freezer, including the correct proportions of the rock salt and chopped ice needed to yield a smooth, creamy ice cream.

Then, sadly enough, modern manufacturing plants sprang up and the old-fashioned hand cranked freezer fell into disuse. Every town soon boasted an "Ice Cream Parlor," and the manufacturers offered innumerable varieties of ice cream, packaged in every manner of carton.

But now, happily, newer and newer kitchen appliances feature ice cream freezers for home use. There are freezers that churn ice cream with the flick of an electric switch. There are freezers that turn smoothly while placed inside refrigerator, with the cord attached to a switch outside the door. And with the modern refrigerator that produces ice cubes in endless quantities the hardest part of freezing homemade ice cream has been simplified.

But the purists still demand hand-churned ice cream. And no matter how inventive the designer, the old-fashioned dasher is still the integral part of making perfect ice cream. And the little girl who asked what a dasher is will grow up and use a modern electric ice cream freezer which will be identical with her grandmother's White Mountain Ice Cream Freezer.

The home cooks have become as inventive as the manufacturers and the number of recipes for homemade ice cream comprises a long list. But great as the number is, all ice cream recipes are classified into three groups: (1) Churned ice cream, (2) Churned Ices and Sherbets, (3) Still-frozen Ice Creams. And with modern home freezers, still-frozen ice creams may be stored in the freezer compartment where they are "still-frozen."

The churned ice cream mixtures are prepared from a custard base, or from sweetened cream, flavoring and fruits or berries, such as strawberries. The ever-popular vanilla ice cream, when prepared from sweetened cream and vanilla extract, is called Philadelphia Ice Cream, and when prepared with a custard base Frozen Custard.

The churned water ices and sherbets are prepared with a syrup base, usually a water ice flavoured with fruit juices. A variant is the very popular old-fashioned milk sherbet, made with milk or buttermilk, and flavored with lemon juice.

The still-frozen ice cream is the richest mixture of all, depending upon a great quantity of heavy cream for its smoothness. Belonging to this classification are, the Bombes, Mousses, Parfaits, and Bisques, including the well-liked

Bisque Tortoni, named after its Italian creator, Señor Tortoni, who was world-famous for his ice cream delicacies.

In today's authentic Italian restaurants, Bisque Tortoni is always a featured dessert. For it makes little difference in the long history of haute cuisine what new inventions the chefs create; basically the most delectable recipes may be traced back to earlier days.

This becomes very apparent to twentieth-century housewives when they prepare homemade Sherbets, Ices, Ice Creams and Mousses in their ultramodern kitchen. For once again, the basic preparation and precautions remain identical to those observed in the old days.

Churned Ice Creams

Hints for Making Ice Cream

(1) Simmer custard base over hot (not boiling) water. This also holds true for scalding cream.

(2) Always strain the cooked custard and/or scalded cream through a fine wire sieve or a clean, dampened piece of cheesecloth.

(3) Stir the cooked custard occasionally while it is cooling. This prevents a film forming on top.

(4) Add ⅛ teaspoon salt to ice cream mixtures.

(5) Always scald the ice cream freezer before pouring in mixture, allow it to cool after scalding.

APRICOT ICE CREAM

2 cups dried apricots, firmly packed	3 egg yolks
Cold water to cover	1 quart of cream
½ to ¾ cup sugar	⅛ teaspoon salt
	1 teaspoon almond extract

Rinse the apricots in cold water, cover with fresh cold water and simmer over low heat until very soft. Add the sugar and stir until sugar is dissolved. Pour off ½ cup of the syrup. Rub the apricots through a sieve. Set aside to cool. Taste, and add more sugar if needed. Beat the yolks until thick. Slowly add the hot syrup. Cook over hot water until the mixture clings to the spoon. Cool and combine with the apricot purée and stir well. Add the cream, salt and flavoring. Freeze.

Variation
Substitute one pint of whipped cream for the cream, pack and freeze without churning.

BANANA ICE CREAM

Prepare Vanilla Ice Cream I (p. 150)
Add peeled, thinly sliced bananas to the cooled mixture before freezing.

CARAMEL ICE CREAM

Vanilla Ice Cream I (p. 150)

1 cup sugar	1 quart table cream

While the vanilla ice cream base is cooking, pour the cup of sugar into a small skillet and stir constantly until it carmelizes and liquefies. Immediately add it to the hot mixture and stir well. Strain through a wire sieve and set aside to cool. When cold, add the cream and freeze.

CHOCOLATE ICE CREAM

I	II
1 pint milk	2 to 3 squares unsweetened
1 cup sugar	chocolate
1/8 teaspoon salt	2 tablespoons sugar
1/4 cup flour	1 tablespoon boiling water
2 eggs, well-beaten	1/2 cup sugar
1 teaspoon vanilla extract	1 quart table cream

Prepare I as in Vanilla Ice Cream I. While this is cooking, melt the chocolate over hot (not boiling) water. Add the sugar and water, stir until smooth and glossy. Add to the first mixture and stir until well blended. Strain through a cheesecloth or a wire sieve. Set aside to cool, stir occasionally. When cold, add the sugar and cream, blend well and freeze.

COFFEE ICE CREAM

Prepare Vanilla Ice Cream I.

While the vanilla ice cream base is cooking, add one cup very strong coffee. Proceed as above. When the cream is added, taste and add 1/4 to 1/2 cup of sugar, if needed.

Variation

1½ cups table cream
1½ to 2 cups sugar
2 tablespoons cornstarch
¼ cup cold milk

1 cup strong coffee
1½ cups whipping cream,
 whipped to a froth

Scald the cream, add the sugar and the cornstarch dissolved in the milk, stir until the sugar is dissolved and the mixture slightly thickened. Add the coffee and simmer for 1 minute. Cool completely, fold in the whipping cream and freeze.

LEMON ICE CREAM

1½ cups sugar
1 cup water
Juice 2 lemons (4 tablespoons)

4 egg yolks, well-beaten
1½ pints table cream

Combine sugar, water and lemon juice to make syrup. Then proceed as in Apricot Ice Cream.

MACAROON ICE CREAM

Vanilla Ice Cream I (p. 150)

1½ dozen dry macaroons

¼ cup white wine

Roll the macaroons into crumbs, stir into the cool ice cream mixture, stir in the wine and freeze.

PEACH ICE CREAM

1 pint table cream
½ cup sugar
⅛ teaspoon salt
1 quart ripe peaches

½ cup sugar
1 tablespoon lemon juice
*1 pint whipping cream & 1
  teaspoon almond extract*

Scald the cream, add ½ cup sugar and salt, and stir until
sugar is dissolved. Strain through wire sieve or cheesecloth.
Set aside to cool.

Peel the peaches,* and cut into small pieces, but do not
mash. Sprinkle with the ½ cup sugar and lemon juice.
Cover and refrigerate for several hours.

Combine all ingredients and freeze.

* Canned peaches may be used or frozen sliced peaches, but the
fresh, ripe peaches are the best.

PEACH ICE CREAM II

1 quart cooked soft custard
*1 teaspoon vanilla or almond
  extract*

1 quart ripe peaches
¼ cup sugar
1 tablespoon lemon juice

Proceed as in Recipe **I**

RUM ICE CREAM

1835

1 quart milk
½ pound sugar
½ pint light rum

½ pint brandy
1½ pints heavy cream
1 teaspoon grated nutmeg

Pour milk over sugar and liquors. Let stand one hour. Stir in cream, add nutmeg and freeze.

20th-Century Variation

Add 1 cup of golden raisins soaked in the liquors for 2 to 3 hours.

STRAWBERRY ICE CREAM

Doubtless God could have made a better berry, but doubtless God never did. DR. BOTELER *The strawberry*

One quart fresh strawberries	*⅛ teaspoon salt*
One pint sugar	*One quart whipping cream*

Wash the strawberries in lukewarm water, lift out with fingers or slotted spoon and drop into a bowl of cold water. Lift out and drain on paper toweling. Hull the berries and mash together with the sugar. Let stand at least one hour. Add the salt to the cream, add the cream slowly, stir well and freeze.

STRAWBERRY ICE CREAM SURPRISE

1880

One of the best-known writers of cookbooks and household management in the late nineteenth century was Miss Maria Parloa. Her books enjoyed wide popularity and a number of the old receipts are still very popular today. One of these is Strawberry Ice Cream Surprise, which is made as follows:

Philadelphia Ice Cream
  (p. 152)
½ cup white wine or rum
1 to 1½ quarts strawberries

1 cup sugar
1 dozen whole, large straw-
  berries

Add the wine or rum to the ice cream mixture before freezing. Wash, hull, dry and crush the berries, sprinkle with the sugar. When the ice cream is frozen, remove the dasher and swirl the mixture to the sides of the freezer. Pour in the berries and cover over with ice cream. Replace the cover and let stand one or more hours. At serving time, turn out on a large, well-chilled dessert platter. And, adds Miss Parloa, "garnish the base, if you please, with strawberries." In the same chapter Miss Parloa presents a receipt for a bombe glacé, using 18 egg yolks.

VANILLA ICE CREAM

1 pint milk
1 pint cream
1 cup sugar
1 tablespoon flour

⅛ teaspoon salt
3 eggs, well beaten
1 tablespoon vanilla extract

Scald the milk over hot (not boiling) water. Mix one-half cup of the sugar with the flour and salt. Stir until well blended. Add to the eggs and beat until thick. Pour a little of the hot milk over and return to heat. Simmer until well thickened, stirring frequently. Set aside to cool. Stir occasionally to prevent a skin forming on top. Add the remaining one-half cup of sugar and the cream. Beat the mixture, add the vanilla flavoring. A pure vanilla extract is essential for all ice creams flavored with vanilla. The imitations are unsatisfactory.

When thoroughly cold, freeze. Note: Read directions on freezer carefully before using it for first time.

VANILLA ICE CREAM II

1 quart milk	⅛ teaspoon salt
4 egg yolks	4 egg whites, stiffly beaten
1 cup sugar	1 pint whipping cream
1 teaspoon cornstarch	1 tablespoon vanilla extract

Scald the milk over hot (not boiling) water. Beat the egg yolks and sugar together until thick. Dissolve the cornstarch in a bit of cold milk to make a paste. Add to egg and sugar mixture. Pour a little of the hot milk over, and return to heat. Cook over low heat until smooth and thickened, stirring constantly. Strain through a coarse wire sieve. Set aside to cool. Whip the cream (or not) add the flavoring and fold in the egg whites. Stir the two mixtures together and freeze.

VANILLA ICE CREAM III

Philadelphia Ice Cream

This favorite old-time recipe has always been known as Philadelphia Ice Cream. It has never been improved upon for smoothness and flavor.

1 quart table cream, scalded*
1 cup sugar
⅛ teaspoon salt

1 to 2 tablespoons vanilla extract

* A richer ice cream is prepared by using half table cream and half whipping cream. Many good cooks prefer to scald just a portion of the cream for vanilla ice cream.

Variations

Chocolate. Melt 2 to 4 squares unsweetened chocolate with 1 cup milk, over hot (not boiling) water. When the chocolate is melted, strain through cheesecloth and set aside to cool. Stir into the ice cream mix and freeze.

Fruit Ice Creams. Any finely cut-up fresh fruit or berries, with vanilla ice cream as a base, make delicious ice creams. Use two to three cups of the fruit to one quart of cream.

Still-Frozen Ice Creams

SEÑOR TORTONI'S BISQUE

Syrup

1 cup sugar	¾ cup water

Simmer over low heat, stirring constantly, until sugar is dissolved. Continue to simmer, without stirring, until the syrup spins a thread (236° on a candy thermometer).

Mixture

4 egg yolks	½ cup almond macaroon
⅛ teaspoon salt	crumbs
2 tablespoons rum	1½ pints whipping cream,
	whipped

Beat the egg yolks and salt until very thick. Slowly add the hot syrup (very slowly—this is important) and continue beating until the mixture forms high peaks. Set aside to cool completely, but do not refrigerate. Add the rum, crumbs and fold in the cream. Do not overbeat the cream. Spoon the mixture into the small fluted paper cups which are traditional for this dessert. Freeze (well covered) in the freezer at 0° temperature.) Garnish with glacé cherries or angelica or sprinkle with finely ground almonds, the classic topping.

Variation: Chocolate Bisque

Add 1⅛ cup fine quality cocoa to the sugar syrup before cooking.

COFFEE MOUSSE

4 egg yolks
½ to ¾ cup sugar
½ cup very strong coffee (hot)
⅛ teaspoon salt

1 cup whipping cream, whipped
4 egg whites, stiffly beaten
1 teaspoon vanilla extract

Beat the egg yolks until thick. Add the sugar gradually and beat until the mixture falls from the spoon in a ribbon. Slowly stir in the hot coffee and simmer over hot (not boiling) water for just a minute or two. Let cool completely. Stir in the cream and salt and fold in the egg whites and flavoring. Pour into a freezer container, cover tightly and freeze at 0° temperature.

FROZEN CABINET PUDDING

1 pint soft custard
2 dozen stale ladyfingers
   (broken into small pieces)
1 cup golden raisins

¼ cup rum or white wine
1 pint whipping cream,
   whipped to a light froth

Pour the hot (strained) custard over the ladyfingers and the raisins. Stir well and set aside to cool. When cold, add the cream and the wine. Freeze as usual. When firm, turn into a melon mould, rinsed with cold water. Sprinkle bottom and sides of mould with raisins; pack the mixture in solidly. Cover and let stand in freezer for an hour or more.
Turn out on well-chilled dessert platter. Garnish with candied cherries or marrons glacé.

NESSELRODE PUDDING

This classic, rich dessert was created by Monsieur Mouy, Chef d' Cuisine to Le Comte de Nesselrode, diplomat at the Russian Court for forty years. The dessert created such a culinary furor that the famous chef, Carême, is said to have been very jealous over its success and quarreled with Muoy. The original receipt is rich beyond all modern tastes.

The ingredients included chestnut purée, a rich custard base, currants and raisins cooked in syrup, a generous quantity of liquers and finished off with whipped cream; the luscious concoction was then frozen. Today's adaptation is a poor copy of the original, but is considered one of the more popular sweets.

1 pint soft custard
1 cup puree of chestnuts
¼ cup candied orange peel
¼ cup candied cherries

½ cup each: currants, raisins*
½ cup Malaga wine
1 pint whipping cream,
*   whipped*

* Soak the currants and raisins in hot water to swell. Drain on paper toweling and cool before proceeding with mixing the pudding.

Let the custard cool thoroughly. Cover the currants, raisins, candied peel and cherries with Malaga wine. Combine all ingredients and line a two-quart ice cream mold with the mixture. Cover the top with wax paper. Fasten lid of mold tightly. Place in freezer for 24 hours. Turn out on large platter and serve with Marrons in Syrup.

STRAWBERRY MOUSSE

Prepare the mixture for Bisque Tortoni, omitting the macaroon crumbs and the rum. Add 1 pint thick crushed strawberries and increase the whipped cream to one quart.

VANILLA MOUSSE

1 pint table cream	*1¼ cups sugar*
2 tablespoons gelatine	*1 pint whipping cream,*
¼ cup cold water	*whipped*
⅛ teaspoon salt	*1 tablespoon vanilla extract*
1 tablespoon lemon juice	*2 egg whites, stiffly beaten*

Scald the cream, add the gelatin softened in the cold water, stir in the salt, lemon juice and sugar. Cool, stirring frequently, in pan of ice water.

Fold in the cream, flavoring and egg whites.

Pack in a freezer container, tightly covered and "still-freeze" in the freezer at 0° temperature.

This is a first-rate base for rich fruit, caramel or chocolate sauces.

Water Ices and Sherbets

The classic proportions for a Water Ice: four parts liquid to one part sugar, otherwise the mixture will not freeze. Chefs de cuisine prepare a hot syrup of the water and sugar, before adding the purée of fruit.

APRICOT WATER ICE

This mixture requires an equal proportion of the sugar syrup and the apricot pulp. Dried apricots, cooked until soft and pureed, are an excellent choice for this water ice.

4 cups sugar syrup
(4 cups water,
1 cup sugar)

4 cups cooked apricot purée
½ cup lemon juice

Freeze according to directions.

BUTTERMILK SHERBET

1 pint cultured buttermilk
1 cup sugar
1 cup canned crushed pineapple
1 teaspoon lemon extract

1 envelope unflavored gelatine
¼ cup cold water
3 egg whites, stiffly beaten

Combine the buttermilk and sugar, stir well, slowly stir in the pineapple and extract. Cover and refrigerate for several hours. Sprinkle gelatine over the cold water, stir and let soften. Place over hot water and stir until syrupy. Stir into the chilled buttermilk mixture. Pour into refrigerator tray and freeze until firm, remove from tray, pour into well-chilled bowl, beat quickly, fold in the egg whites, return to tray and freeze.

LEMON ICE

1 cup sugar	*1 teaspoon grated lemon rind*
4 cups water	*¼ teaspoon salt*
Simmer over low heat for 5 minutes. Cool and add:	*¾ cup lemon juice*

LEMON SHERBET

Delicious

Juice three large lemons	*1 quart milk*
1½ cups sugar	*⅛ teaspoon salt*

Combine the lemon juice and sugar, let stand until sugar is dissolved. Add the salt and slowly add the milk, stirring constantly. The milk may curdle, but it will smooth out in the freezing.

Variation
Substitute 1 cup whipping cream for 1 cup milk. This is unusually good.

ORANGE ICE

1 cup sugar
2 cups water

2 cups fresh (not canned) orange juice
1 tablespoon grated orange rind

Simmer sugar and water over low heat and stir until sugar is dissolved. Cook for 5 minutes, then add orange juice and rind.

PINEAPPLE ICE

1 cup sugar

4 cups water

Simmer over low heat, stir until sugar is dissolved and cook for 5 minutes. Cool and add:

1 cup crushed, drained pineapple

¼ cup lemon juice

RASPBERRY OR STRAWBERRY ICE

1 package quick-frozen red raspberries or sliced strawberries
1 cup sugar
2 cups water

Thaw and simmer berries over low heat for 5 minutes. Strain to remove seeds. Measure 2 cups of thick juice. Set aside.

Simmer sugar and water over low heat, stir until sugar is dissolved and cook for 5 minutes.

Cool and mix with fruit juice. Add 1 tablespoon lemon juice.

Baked Puddings

Hot puddings were regularly served in earlier days when thrifty, substantial meals were the custom. The puddings ranged from simple to heavy, rich ones. But the writers of cookbooks took it for granted that their readers were well informed, as the following example indicates. "Hunter's Pudding . . . Take currents, flour, suet and raisins, add a sufficiency of milk to make a batter."

Apples, currants—spelled today with an "a," not "e"— and raisins were plentiful, as was cornmeal. Many of the desserts depended on apples as an ingredient, as is seen in the following examples.

Notes on Puddings

1. When cooking a custard base, or a scalded milk base for a cornstarch pudding, the milk or custard should always be strained through a piece of clean, dampened cheesecloth, or through a very fine wire sieve.

2. A custard mixture, with the eggs added, must be stirred constantly, or it will curdle. If the water boils it will also curdle.

3. If it is a flour or a cornstarch mixture, it may be stirred frequently.

4. All of these mixtures should be stirred while cooling to prevent a film forming on the top.

APPLE COBS

Preheat oven to 375°　　　　　*A baking pan.*

Pastry crust	*⅛ teaspoon allspice*
¼ teaspoon cinnamon	*6 baking apples*
½ teaspoon nutmeg	*6 tablespoon strained honey*

Sift the spices with the flour before making the pastry crust. Roll out the crust and cut into squares according to the size of the apples. The crust must be large enough to cover the apples completely and fold over from corner to corner at the top.

Core and peel the apples, place each apple in center of pastry square. Fill cavity of apples with the honey. Bake about 30 minutes in a buttered pan. Serve with Brandy Sauce (p. 216).

APPLE COBBLER

The old-fashioned hearty hot dessert known as an Apple Cobbler stands near the top of the list of favorite desserts. As is true of so many of our dishes, the arguments over the correct nomenclature continue to fly. But as a general rule, a Cobbler is made with fruit or berries, covered with a rich biscuit dough and baked in the oven until the fruit is cooked and the crust golden brown. The dessert is also prepared with the crust on the bottom and the fruit on top. In some parts of the country this dessert is called a Deep-Dish pie. The fruit is covered with a tender flaky pie crust and then baked.

While the apple reigns as our most popular fruit, the Cobblers and the Deep-Dish pies are also delicious when prepared with other fruits and berries in season. These include peaches, plums, apricots, pears, strawberries, blackberries, red raspberries and blueberries.

Preheat oven to 425°	*Two-quart baking dish*
2 to 3 cups peeled, thinly sliced tart cooking apples	*½ teaspoon cinnamon or grated nutmeg*
¼ teaspoon salt	*Baking Powder Biscuit Dough (p. 35)*
1 tablespoon flour	*A few tablespoons soft butter*
½ to ¾ cup sugar	

Butter the baking dish well, and sprinkle bottom with sugar. Combine the salt, flour, sugar and cinnamon (or nutmeg), and stir well. Arrange the apples in over-lapping layers and sprinkle each layer with the sugar mixture. Add bits of the soft butter to each layer. Cover with the crust, and make two or three two-inch slashes in the top to allow the steam to escape. Bake for 10 minutes and then reduce the heat to 375°. Bake until apples are tender. Serve with cream or Hard Sauce or any other sweet sauce.

CHERRY COBBLER

If sour red cherries are used—and they are by far the best—simmer them in a sugar syrup for 10 to 15 minutes. Allow the cherries to cool before covering with the crust.

APPLE CRISP

(Brown Betty)

Preheat oven to 375°　　　　*Two-quart baking dish*

1 quart sliced tart, cooking apples	*¼ teaspoon salt*
½ cup stale cake crumbs or bread crumbs	*½ teaspoon cinnamon*
	¼ teaspoon all spice
¾ to 1 cup brown sugar, firmly packed	*1 tablespoon flour*
	Soft butter

Wash, core, peel and slice apples. Arrange in a well-buttered baking dish. Combine the remaining ingredients, and spread over the apples. If the apples are very dry, pour one tablespoon of water over them. Omit flour if a crisper pudding is preferred. Bake until apples are tender. Serve warm with cream, or arrange in alternate layers.

APPLE FRITTERS

Fritter Batter

Heat fat in deep-frying kettle to 370°	1 tablespoon sugar
1 cup sifted all-purpose flour	1 egg yolk, well-beaten
1 teaspoon baking powder	¾ cup milk
¼ teaspoon salt	1 tablespoon melted butter
	3 or 4 cooking apples

Sift dry ingredients together, add egg yolk, milk and butter. Stir together quickly.

Core and peel apples, cut in slices. Dip one piece of fruit in the batter with a long-handled slotted spoon. Lower it into the hot fat. If the batter slides off the fruit, add a small amount of extra flour to the batter. Test one more slice of apple in the batter and fry. The fritters should cook in 5 to 7 minutes. Drain on paper towels. Sprinkle with powdered sugar and serve hot.

Bananas, peaches, apricots may all be fried in this same batter.

CHERRY TOAST

Preheat oven to 375°	One-quart baking dish
6 slices toast, crusts trimmed	⅛ teaspoon salt
1 (No. 2) can pitted sour cherries	1 tablespoon flour
½ cup sugar	One 2-inch stick cinnamon

Butter the toast, cut in fingers and arrange a layer in the buttered baking dish. Drain the cherries, measure the juice. Add cold water to make two cups of liquid. Mix the sugar, salt and flour with the juice, add the cinnamon stick, simmer over low heat until slightly thickened. Remove the cinnamon. Add the cherries, and set aside to cool. Arrange alternate layers of the toast fingers with the cherry mixture until all is used. The top layer should be the toast fingers. Bake until golden brown (about 10 minutes). Serve with cream, custard sauce or whipped cream, or if a portion of the cooked cherry sauce is left over, serve the extra cherry sauce with the pudding.

CHOCOLATE PUDDING

Preheat oven to 400°   *Two-quart baking dish*

1 quart milk, scalded   ½ cup soft bread crumbs
4 squares unsweetened chocolate   1 teaspoon vanilla extract
¼ teaspoon salt   4 eggs, well-beaten
1 cup sugar

Scald milk in upper part of double boiler, over hot (not boiling) water. Strain through a piece of clean, dampened cheesecloth. Melt the chocolate, combine with salt, sugar and bread crumbs. Pour the milk over and let stand for 5 minutes. Add the eggs and flavoring, stir well and bake in buttered pudding dish until a silver knife inserted in pudding comes out dry, about 30 minutes. Serve hot with cream.

Variation

For a more delicate pudding, beat the eggs separately. Beat the egg whites until stiff and fold in at the last minute, or make a meringue and cover the top of the pudding (Meringue, p. 111).

BAKED DATE TAPIOCA PUDDING

1888

In the nineteenth century, sago or, as it was usually named, pearl tapioca was the basis for many baked puddings. The large grains were coarse and had to be soaked overnight, which caused them to double in or triple in bulk. Today, this product is difficult to find, as a modern tapioca, Minute, has replaced it. As its name implies, it is a matter of minutes to prepare the desserts, which are still delicious light puddings.

Preheat oven to 350°   *Two-quart baking dish*

½ cup Minute tapioca   1 cup sugar
5 cups cold water   2 tablespoons lemon juice
⅛ teaspoon salt   2 cups pitted dates, cut in pieces

Combine the tapioca, water, salt and sugar. Let stand for 10 to 15 minutes, stir occasionally. Simmer over low heat until it comes to a full, rolling boil. Add the lemon juice and dates. Stir and pour into baking dish. Bake for 15 to 20 minutes. Five minutes before the pudding is done, sprinkle the topping over and bake for 5 minutes longer. Serve hot, with cream.

Topping

1 cup soft, fresh bread crumbs   ¼ cup blanched, sliced al-
¼ teaspoon salt   monds
¼ cup melted butter

Combine the ingredients and sprinkle over the pudding.

Variations

1. Apple Tapioca. Substitute 2 cups of peeled, thinly sliced tart apples for the cut-up dates. Bake until the apples are tender, cool slightly and dust the top of the pudding with a sprinkling of nutmeg or cinnamon. Bread crumbs may be omitted, and bits of soft butter substituted. Serve warm with cream.

2. Sliced, peeled plums, peaches, or other raw fruit, or pitted sour cherries may be used instead of dates.

MOOST AYE SAVE-ALL PUDDING

The old cookbooks gave receipts that required far longer cooking than modern recipes demand. One sixteenth-century receipt advises, "If your fire is very fierce, mind and stir the puddings every now and then." "Do not bake pears for more than six hours." An old-time pudding with a delightful name was called a "MOOST AYE SAVE-ALL PUDDING."

Preheat oven to 350°.   *One-quart casserole*

½ cup jam
2 cups soft bread crumbs
½ cup butter, cut into bits
½ cup sugar

2 eggs, well beaten
½ cup milk
Grated rind and juice of 1 lemon

Cover bottom of casserole with the jam. Combine the bread crumbs, butter and sugar. Mix eggs, milk, juice and rind together and pour over the bread crumbs. Let stand 15 minutes. Bake in a buttered casserole for ½ hour. Serve with cream or soft custard.

NEW ENGLAND INDIAN PUDDING

19th century

Preheat oven to 300°   *2-quart baking dish*

1 quart milk, scalded   ¼ *cup sugar*
(set aside ¼ cup)   *1 teaspoon cinnamon or all-*
¼ *cup yellow cornmeal*   *spice*
¼ *teaspoon salt*   ¼ *cup butter*
½ *cup dark molasses*

Butter the baking dish. Sift the corn meal over the scalded milk. Simmer over hot water until the mixture thickens; about 20 minutes. Combine the remaining ingredients (with exception of the cold milk). Add the hot mixture and stir until the mixture is well blended. Pour into the baking dish. Set in a pan of hot water. Gently pour the ¼ cup milk over the top of the pudding. Bake for 1 to 1½ hours. A crust will form on top and the center will be soft. Serve warm with cream or a scoop of vanilla ice cream.

Variations

1. Add 1 cup golden raisins.
2. Add 2 cups peeled, sliced tart apples. Reduce milk to 1 pint.

SWEET POTATO PUDDING

1880

Preheat oven to 350°   *3-quart round casserole*

½ cup butter   6 eggs, well beaten
1 cup sugar   1 pound sweet potatoes, boiled,
¼ teaspoon salt   peeled, mashed
½ teaspoon grated nutmeg

Cream butter. Add the sugar gradually and beat until light
and fluffy. Add salt and nutmeg. Add eggs and beat well.
Add potatoes and beat until thoroughly blended. Pour into
well-buttered casserole. Place in pan of hot water and bake
until a silver knife inserted in center comes out dry (about
1 hour). Serve with pitcher of cream.

Steamed Puddings

A rich, hearty steamed pudding was one of the traditional
desserts in grandmother's day. The flaming plum pudding
with hard sauce served at the end of Christmas dinner may
be remembered by many grandparents today, even though
years have elapsed since it has been traditionally served.
Our tastes have turned to lighter, more delicate fare.

However, another reason for the loss of popularity of the
steamed pudding is the inordinate amount of time it took
to prepare. According to one writer, the batter had to
"bubble and steam for five hours."

The writers of the early cookbooks had great faith in their readers, as they just assumed the housewives knew all. One receipt, for example, ran as follows: "A receipt for a Nice Flour Pudding . . . One dozen eggs, two quarts of milk, flour to a batter, pour in bag and boil four hours. Two pounds of currents is a great improvement."

Another writer even went to the trouble to quote prices for ingredients. Quoth she, "A Black Pudding . . . Take a five cent Baker's loaf and a quart of blackberries."

Today's recipes frequently replace the old favorite, chopped suet, with butter and or sour cream. The following recipe for Berry Pudding uses butter entirely.

PHOEBE'S BERRY PUDDING

¼ cup butter
1 cup sugar
1 egg, well beaten
¾ cup milk
1 teaspoon vanilla extract
1½ cups sifted all-purpose
  flour

2 teaspoons baking powder
½ teaspoon salt
1 cup canned, fresh or frozen
  blueberries or blackberries

Cream butter, add the sugar gradually and beat until light and fluffy. Add the egg. Resift the dry ingredients. Add milk and flavoring, alternately with the flour, beginning and ending with the flour. If the berries are fresh, rinse and dry well before adding. Sprinkle lightly with a bit of the flour and stir in. If the berries are canned or frozen, drain, but add the milk carefully to be sure not to have too much liquid.

Custard Cup method: grease and sprinkle with sugar. Steam at full boil for an hour.

Pressure Cooker Method

Grease the inside of a metal mold and sprinkle with sugar. Fill the mold ⅔ full and cover tightly. Always reduce the heat after steaming, then remove from heat and allow the pudding to cool slightly. Uncover and complete the cooling in the pudding mold.

The basic directions are the same, no matter what utensil or appliance is used. Always butter the mold well. Fill two-thirds full only to allow for swelling. Always tie down tightly fitted cover with wax paper.

If unaccustomed to a pressure cooker, read the directions of the manufacturer. In using a large steamer, pour the boiling water halfway up the sides. Keep the boiling water at this level, and always keep a space between the wall of the kettle and the wall of the pudding mold.

Always turn the warm pudding out on a warm platter and serve on warm plates.

CABINET PUDDING

One-quart pudding mold

Thin slices bread, finger size	*1 pint light cream*
½ cup raisins	*1 teaspoon vanilla extract*
½ cup sugar	*½ teaspoon nutmeg*
2 eggs, well beaten	

Butter the bottom and sides of the baking dish. Line with the bread, lightly and sparingly buttered. Cover the bottom with the raisins and press down lightly.

Beat the custard ingredients together. Strain through a fine wire sieve or cheesecloth. Carefully pour over the bread, being careful not to loosen it from the sides.

Fill the mold ⅔ full. Let stand for 30 minutes. Cover with wax paper and tie securely. Steam for one hour. Turn out on warm platter and serve with Vanilla or Orange Sauce (p. 223).

CHOCOLATE PUDDING

One-quart pudding mold

2 eggs, well-beaten	½ cup sifted all-purpose flour
1 cup milk	2 squares unsweetened chocolate, melted
1 cup sugar	
⅛ teaspoon salt	1 teaspoon vanilla extract

Butter the pudding mold. Combine the eggs, milk, sugar and salt. Add the flour gradually, beating well after each addition. Cool chocolate slightly and stir into the mixture until well blended. Add the flavoring and pour into the pudding mold according to directions for steamed puddings. Steam according to directions for the steamer method used.

DATE PUDDING

Two-quart pudding mold

3 cups sifted all-purpose flour	½ cup butter
½ cup sugar	¼ cup molasses
1 teaspoon baking powder	½ pound pitted dates, cut into bits
¼ teaspoon salt	
½ cup lard	¼ to ½ cup whiskey

Resift flour with dry ingredients. Cut in shortening with pastry blender or two knives. Combine the molasses and dates. Pour whiskey over and let stand for 30 minutes. Combine mixtures and beat well. Butter the mold according to directions and steam in pressure cooker.

FRUIT DUMPLINGS

Dumplings were a standby for dessert in pioneer days. Light, feathery, with a fruit sauce, they are easy to prepare. The one secret is to keep tightly covered while steaming, and not peek to see if they are done.

Dumpling Batter

1 cup sifted all-purpose flour	*2 tablespoons butter or lard*
2 teaspoons baking powder	*½ cup milk*
½ teaspoon salt	*1 teaspoon vanilla extract*
¼ cup sugar	

Resift the flour with the dry ingredients. Cut in the shortening with two knives or a pastry blender. Stir in the milk all at once. The mixture must be thick enough to drop by spoonfuls on top of boiling liquid.

The Boiling Liquid

Use fresh berries, pitted cherries or peeled, sliced apples, peaches or peeled, halved apricots. If out of season, canned peaches, apricots or sour cherries make good dumplings.

Choose a fairly shallow saucepan, with a wide mouth and

a tightly-fitted cover. Fill with the berries or fruit and cover with cold water, add sugar as needed and simmer over low heat until the fruit is nearly cooked. Bring to boiling point and drop the dumpling batter over the top in spoonfuls. The dumplings will float. Do not over-crowd. Allow room for the dumplings to swell and expand. Cover the pan quickly. Set the timer for exactly 12 minutes and do not peek, or the dumplings will fall. Lift dumplings out with a slotted spoon, add the fruit sauce and serve at once.

ORANGE PUDDING

Two-quart mold

¼ cup butter
¼ cup sifted all-purpose flour
1 cup light cream, scalded
1 teaspoon lemon extract
1 tablespoon grated orange rind

¼ cup strained orange juice
½ cup sugar
6 egg yolks
6 egg whites

Melt the butter, add the flour and stir over low heat until smooth and bubbly. Add the cream and stir until thickened. Strain and cool.

Combine the extract, the rind, juice and sugar. Let stand a few minutes. Beat the egg yolks until thick and lemon-colored, add the juice mixture and combine with the cooled milk mixture.

Fold in the stiffly beaten egg whites and pour into the buttered mold. Steam for 30 minutes. If a pressure cooker is used, follow the manufacturer's directions.

PUDDING IN A MELON MOLD

Heavy tin melon mold

1 cup mixed dried fruits:
citron (*sliced very thin*), currants, raisins
2 cups dry sponge cake crumbs

4 eggs, well-beaten
½ cup sugar
¼ teaspoon salt
3 cups milk

Butter the mold generously. Press a layer of the fruit on the bottom and sides of the mold. Sprinkle cake crumbs over the fruit, using the bowl of a spoon. Continue with fruit and crumbs alternately until all are used. Beat the custard ingredients together. Strain through a fine wire sieve or dampened cheesecloth. Carefully pour over the fruit mixture. Cover with wax paper and tie securely. Secure cover and refrigerate for two or more hours. Steam 1½ hours. Turn out on warm platter and serve with Brandy sauce, (p. 216).

SUET PUDDING

A well-tested family receipt from the 19th century, equally good in the 20th century.

Two-quart mold

½ cup finely chopped suet
2 cups sifted all-purpose flour
2 teaspoons baking powder
½ teaspoon salt
½ teaspoon each:
cloves, cinnamon,*
nutmeg, ginger

½ cup milk
½ teaspoon soda
2 eggs, well-beaten
½ cup dark molasses
1 cup raisins
½ cup currants

* For a spicier flavor, double the amount of cinnamon.

Combine suet with sifted flour, baking powder, salt and spices. Dissolve the soda in the milk, combine with the eggs, molasses and dried fruits.* Stir all ingredients together until well blended. Pour into buttered mold and proceed according to directions.

* For best results, rinse all dried fruits in cold water, dry on paper toweling and dust lightly with flour. Shake off any excess flour. Fruit must be bone-dry.

Frostings and Fillings

*"The pleasures of the table are enjoyed by
all who possess good health."*

The variety of frostings, toppings and cake fillings run the
gamut from very simple ones, such as jelly or jam spread
between two layers of cake, to fussy cooked frostings and
rich butter cream frostings and fillings.

Today if the housewife is in a hurry and cannot take time
to prepare a frosting, the markets are filled with prepared
canned frostings, boxed frostings, ready to-spread and boxed
frosting bases, to which the cook adds extra butter. But none
of these equals the frostings, fillings and toppings prepared
at home.

In the old days huge quantities were prepared as seen by
this receipt of 1842 for a frosting: Take ten egg whites, allow
two pounds of sifted loaf sugar. Cut the whites to a high
froth, then add the sugar and beat it steadily, til it will stay
where it is put. This will require two hours at least. Lay it
on the loaves and return it to the oven for fifteen minutes
(See Uncooked Icing, p. 185).

To bake a Wedding Cake the receipt called for: Ten
pounds of flour, sugar and butter, seventy eggs, twelve
pounds of currents and four pounds of raisins. Truly, the
changes in cookery have been many, some for the better,
some for the worse. But in the case of cake frostings, the
change is definitely for the better.

ALMOND TOPPING

½ cup sugar	1 (8 oz.) can almond paste
½ cup water	1 teaspoon almond extract
2 tablespoons finely	
chopped orange peel	

Simmer sugar and water over low heat, stirring constantly until sugar is dissolved. Add the orange peel and continue to simmer for another 5 minutes. Strain out the peel and cool the syrup. Cut the almond paste into small pieces, and slowly add the syrup, beating well after each addition. When the consistency is thick and smooth, cool and spread between cake layers and on top.

Variation

½ cup butter	Orange flavored syrup
1½ to 2 cups 10-X sugar	Almond paste

Cream the butter, add the sugar gradually and beat in the almond paste. Add enough syrup, a spoonful at a time, for spreading consistency.

BOILED FROSTING

2 cups sugar	¼ teaspoon cream of tartar
1 cup cold water	1 teaspoon vanilla, lemon or
½ teaspoon salt	almond extract.
2 egg whites	

Combine sugar and water. Simmer over low heat. Stir until sugar is dissolved, then omit stirring. Cover and simmer for

3 minutes. Uncover and simmer until the syrup spins a thread (240° by a candy thermometer). Do not stir.
Beat the egg whites (and salt) until frothy. Slowly pour the syrup over the whites, beating steadily. When the mixture is thick and smooth, add the cream of tartar and the flavoring. Do not try to make this frosting on a damp, rainy day.

Variation

Add 1 cup grated coconut. This makes a very handsome frosted cake. Sprinkle extra coconut over the top.
For a Lady Baltimore Cake, double the amount for the boiled frosting.

CARAMEL FILLING

*2 cups brown sugar, firmly
   packed*
½ cup light cream

⅛ teaspoon salt
1 tablespoon butter
1 teaspoon vanilla extract

Combine sugar, cream and salt. Simmer over low heat, stirring constantly until sugar is dissolved. Do not stir again. Cook until the syrup spins a thread. Remove from heat, add 1 tablespoon butter and flavoring. Let cool and then beat until spreading consistency. Spread between layers of White Cake.

CHOCOLATE BOILED ICING

Boiled Frosting (½ recipe)
2 to 4 squares unsweetened chocolate

Melt the chocolate over hot (not boiling) water. Set aside to cool. As soon as the frosting is finished, slowly add the melted chocolate, stirring constantly until the desired amount is used. Any unused melted chocolate may be set aside to use at a later date. Simply remelt.

Variation

Frost a cake with any white frosting. Swirl spoonfuls of the melted chocolate over the (hardened) frosting. It will run down the sides and look very dramatic.

CHOCOLATE BUTTER CREAM

½ cup unsalted butter
2 egg yolks
1 pound 10-X sugar
4 squares unsweetened chocolate
Hot liquid:
light cream, strong coffee, or
boiling water

1 or 2 egg yolks
1 teaspoon vanilla extract
¼ teaspoon salt

Cream butter; add the sugar gradually and beat until light and fluffy. Melt the chocolate over hot (not boiling) water. Add the melted chocolate alternately with the hot liquid until the mixture is spreading consistency. Add more sugar if needed. Beat in the egg yolk, the salt, and the flavoring. For easy spreading, dip a long-handled spatula in very hot water, dry quickly and use until the layers are smooth.
The hot liquid should be hot to the touch, but not boiling hot. The strong coffee should be twice the strength (or more) of drinkable coffee.

CHOCOLATE GLAZE FOR PETITS FOURS

4 squares unsweetened chocolate
¼ cup water

Syrup
½ cup sugar
¼ cup water
1 tablespoon butter
¼ cup cream

Melt chocolate and water over hot (not boiling) water. Cook sugar and water until syrupy. Add the chocolate and cook until thickened and smooth. Bring just to boiling point. Add butter and cream and cook until smooth. Cool before pouring over petits fours. Let stand on wire rack and reuse the glaze that drips down. Lay a length of clean wax paper under the cake rack.

If necessary, reheat glaze as it cools and stiffens.

CHOCOLATE GLOSSY FROSTING

½ cup sugar
2 tablespoons cornstarch
⅛ teaspoon salt
½ cup boiling (must be boiling) water

2 squares unsweetened chocolate
2 tablespoons butter
1 teaspoon vanilla (or almond extract if cake is garnished with blanched almonds)

Mix the sugar, cornstarch and salt together. Add the chocolate, (broken into pieces) and the water. Simmer over low heat until smooth and glossy. Add the butter and the flavoring. Spread while warm.

COFFEE CAKE TOPPING

½ cup brown sugar, firmly
    packed
1 tablespoon flour

1 teaspoon cinnamon
2 tablespoons firm butter
½ cup chopped nut meats

Combine first three ingredients and stir until well blended. Cut in butter with pastry blender or two knives, until mixture is consistency of coarse corn-meal. Stir in the nut meats.

CREAM FILLING

2 cups milk
(set aside ½ cup)
¼ cup sugar
4 tablespoons cornstarch

2 eggs, well-beaten
¼ cup soft butter
Favoring, vanilla or brandy

Scald 1½ cups cold milk in upper part of double boiler (over hot, not boiling) water. Add the sugar and stir until dissolved. Mix the cornstarch with the ½ cup cold milk to make a smooth paste. Pour a little of the hot milk over, stir and return to double boiler. Cook, stirring constantly, until the mixture is smooth and thick. Pour a little over the eggs, stir and return to double boiler. Stir until well blended. Cook for 1 minute, add the butter and beat into the mixture. Add 1 teaspoon of any flavoring, or 1 tablespoon of brandy. Remove from heat, and pour into bowl to cool. Stir occasionally as the mixture cools.

GOLDEN FROSTING

3 egg yolks
1½ to 2 cups 10-X sugar
¼ teaspoon salt

1 teaspoon almond extract
Warm cream, if needed

Beat egg yolks until thick and lemon-colored. Add sugar gradually. If too thick, add a little warm cream. If too thin, increase amount of sugar. Add salt and extract.

LADY BALTIMORE CAKE FILLING AND FROSTING

One of the most delicious and most eye-catching of the old cakes was the Lady Baltimore Cake. It was the centerpiece at every tea party. And it is so good it would pay today's housewife to make one for a festive occasion.

The cake itself was a delicate white cake (p. 87). It was the filling that was different.

Filling for Three Layers

Invert the three cake layers. Brush each one lightly with a coating of Simple Syrup (p. 224). Let stand for 30 minutes. Prepare a double recipe of Boiled Frosting. Divide into two bowls. Reserve one bowl of the frosting for the sides and top of the cake. Blend the remaining half of the frosting with:

½ cup golden raisins (or figs)
½ cup finely cut glacé cherries
½ cup finely chopped nut meats

Spread this filling between the layers. Skewer layers with toothpicks to hold firmly. Cover with the top layer and frost the sides and top.

LEMON FILLING FOR SPONGE CAKE

2 tablespoons butter
1 cup sugar
Juice and grated rind

2 lemons
2 eggs, well-beaten

Blend all ingredients, cook over hot water until smooth and thick. Cool and spread between sponge cake layers.

MOCHA FROSTING

½ cup unsalted butter
1 pound (or more) 10-X sugar
½ cup Dutch cocoa
⅛ teaspoon salt

2 to 4 tablespoons double
    strength hot coffee
2 egg yolks

Cream butter; sift the sugar, cocoa and salt together. Add to the butter until it is very stiff. Add the coffee spoonful by spoonful. The consistency of the frosting should be thick enough to spread smoothly. Add one or two egg yolks for a very creamy consistency.

The easiest way to spread this type of frosting is to fill a pitcher with boiling hot water in which to dip the spatula from time to time while spreading the frosting.

The strong coffee should be about 2 tablespoons (coffee measure) to one cup of coffee. Taste and, if not strong enough, make a note for the next time.

ORANGE FROSTING

1 egg white   Grated rind and juice of one
2 cups 10-X sugar   orange*

Beat the egg white until very frothy. Add the sugar gradually and, as it stiffens, add the orange juice and stir well. When the consistency is thick enough to spread, stir in the grated rind.

* While it is true that the juice oranges are better for juice than the navel oranges, the latter has a better rind for thickness and good looks.

Variations
1. An unbeaten egg white may be used in place of the beaten egg white, but the texture will be different.
2. Beat in ¼ cup soft butter when the mixture is thick.

UNCOOKED LEMON ICING

1888 adapted to 1972

2 unbeaten egg whites   Grated rind of ½ lemon
2 to 2½ cups 10-X sugar   Juice one lemon

Let whites stand at room temperature for one hour. Gradually add the sugar, stirring thoroughly. As the mixture stiffens, add the lemon juice drop by drop. When consistency is thick enough to spread easily, add the grated lemon rind.
This frosting is often called Ornamental Icing, as it lends itself to holding candied cherries or blanched almonds firmly in place.

Beverages

Historians who delve into the ancient past to discover the origin of our foods and beverages tell us that the fermentation of grain was stumbled upon by accident, not too long after man learned to plant wheat. He found that the crushed grain, mixed with water and allowed to ferment, made a good beverage.

The origin of fermented liquors is customarily traced back to Egypt and Mesopotamia, and the Old Testament makes many references to wine. But whatever the early discoveries of man may have been, his descendants have gone happily on brewing, distilling, mixing, sampling and bottling.

In the very earliest cookbook which has been handed down to us, *The Art of Cooking* by Apicius, there are many descriptions and receipts for fermented drinks. The early Romans knew Vermouth and many other wines, both red and white. They used honey to sweeten certain drinks and used all manner of herbs and spices. Rose leaves were steeped in wine and used in profusion. A spiced honey wine (which keeps forever) was prepared for traveling. Apicius told how to turn red wine into white by adding egg white to the red wine. He then added, "The white ashes of vine have the same effect."

As the centuries rolled on and the tastes of each generation changed, so did the old receipts for fermented liquor. One receipt was for Mead, a beverage prepared from honey. A receipt was also given for a Methaglin, a "weaker" version of Mead, and for Verjuyce, a potable prepared from unripe grapes or crab apples.

An Elder Wine, which was spiced with ginger and heated in a device known as a "Hooter," was a popular drink. Ale was highly regarded as was Buttered Ale, quaffed with pleasure in the bitter cold of the winter.

Most of the old beverages are no longer made, but a few have survived. In some the changes are imperceptible. In others major changes have occurred, as in the case of the famous Sillabub, which changed completely from a beverage to a wine dessert, still enjoyed today. But its counterpart in some ways, a Posset, has been discarded entirely. Cups and Bowls and Punches are still popular beverages, both alcoholic and nonalcoholic.

In the old records, it is noted that the early colonists included both beer and rum in their long lists of provisions for the sea voyages. And the Founding Fathers liked a glass of wine as well as the "common" man. Indeed, one of the treasures in our archives is the handwritten receipt for beer by George Washington himself. Many receipts for Sillibubs appeared in every one of the early cookbooks. While the spelling changed from century to century, the basic recipe remained.

By the seventeenth century, when the early settlers in the New World had learned of the possibilities for pleasing potables that could be prepared in their own domain, the search for new beverages was on in full stride. Every household of stature had its own stillroom, and the bounty of the hedges and the meadows was used to the fullest to prepare such beverages as Dandelion, Elderberry, Rhubarb and Currant wine, among others. Sloe Gin was prepared from the small, dark fruit of the Blackthorn (sloes). There were Wine Cups, Cider Cups, Claret Cups and Mulled Claret.

And today, at the holiday season, many a bowl of the Bishop's Cup is served. Originally it was an elaborate concoction, with roasted lemons or oranges stuck with whole cloves; and spices, port wine, flambéed to complete the mixture. The Wassail Bowl was also a special holiday treat and the Gossip's Bowl kept pace in popularity. It, too, is served today, with modern variations to please the twentieth-century taste.

SILLABUB

The Encyclopedia of Food gives the following definition of Sillabub: A sillabub is a variously flavored mixture; wine or cider plus cream. The wine turns the cream into a soft curd. The name is taken from the champagne county of Sill or Sille and the syllable "bub" is Elizabethan slang for a bubbly drink. The varied spellings distinguish changes from the sixteenth to eighteenth centuries.

16th century Lemon Sillabubes

Take one quart of cream, 3 quarters of a pound of double refined sugar, and ye juice of 4 lemons with some of ye peel grated into a pint of white wine, and half a pint of Sack. Put all of these in a clean pan and with a wisk keep it stirring all one way for half an hour. Then take off ye froth as it rises and put into your glasses; it is the better for keeping two or three days and it will keep a week.

17th century Whip't Sillibub

Take a pint of white wine and half a pound of good fine suggar & mingle it togeather then put it to a quart of thick raw creame and-stir them togeather and Squoos a leamon into ye wine before ye put it to yecreame, then-take three or four Strong branches of Rosomary and whip it and as the Fraught rises take it off and put it to Sillibub glasses or potts, but be sure ye take nowt of the milke and soe whip it till ye have taken all of itt.

17th century Curd Sillibub

7 oz. sugar	2 wine glasses brandy
Juice and grated rind two lemons	1 pint cream, whipped to a froth
2 wine glasses sherry	

In a large bowl, combine sugar, lemon juice, rind and wine. Pour into glasses, pour cream over it. This will form a curd.

18th century Sillabub

½ pint white wine	Sugar to taste
½ wine glass brandy	1 pint cream
Juice of 1 lemon	

Combine wine, brandy, juice and sugar. Let stand until sugar is dissolved. Add the cream and whip until frothy. Skim off froth and place in dessert glasses. Continue until all is used.

189

Sillabub II

Take fresh double cream, Rhenish wine and Sack, juices and chopped rind of oranges and lemons, plus Orange Flower water. Let stand for two days. A liquid forms at the bottom to be drawn off and flavored with puree of fresh strawberries.

A 15th CENTURY WINE

1 gallon claret or white wine	*1½ oz. nutmeg*
Put therein:	*¼ oz. cloves*
4 oz. ginger	*4 lbs. sugar*

The writer, Gervase Markham, says: "Let stand for 12 hours, then take it, and put into a clean bag made for the purpose, so that the wine may come with good leisure from the spices."

POSSETS

Another beverage which ranked in popularity with the Sillibubs was a concoction known as a Posset. Two fifteenth-century definitions describe a Posset thus:
"A Posset Pot doth contain milk, eggs, sugar and wine" and "A Posset is hot milk curdled by wine or ale. spiced if liked."

ORANGE POSSET

15th century

Juice 3 oranges ⎫
Juice 3 lemons ⎬ *Let stand to make a syrup*
Sugar to sweeten ⎭
1 pint cream or milk
2 eggs

The directions, according to Verral Palgrave's *Complete System of Cookery*, were as follows:
"Pour cream into a clean tea pot and from a height, pour the cream onto the syrup. Drink it with sweetmeats, and blanched almonds."

KING WILLIAM'S POSSET

16th century

10 egg yolks   1 pint ale
1 quart cream   4 egg whites
¼ to ½ cup sugar   Grated nutmeg

Beat egg yolks until thick, add cream and sugar and stir until well mixed. Add the ale and fold in the stiffly beaten egg whites. Pour into a Posset Bowl and sprinkle with nutmeg. This was served as eggnog is served today.

THE GOSSIP'S BOWL

17th century

When roasted crabs hiss in the bowl.

1 quart ale	*½ grated nutmeg*
1 pint wine	*1 dozen crab apples*

Heat the ale and wine, but do not boil. Add the nutmeg and sugar. Wash and dry crab apples, and roast in a very hot oven until the skins burst. Pour the punch into a large bowl and float the apples on the top.

FLIP

The eighteenth century beverage, Flip, was prepared as follows:
Choose a one quart pitcher. Fill it ⅔ full with ale or beer, add sweetening of sugar and water syrup. Fill remainder of pitcher with rum. Stir well with a red-hot poker from the fireplace.

MONKFIASCO PUNCH

18th century

Take the parings of six lemons and as many oranges all pared very thin & put 'em to steep in a gallon of brandy close stop't for 3 or 4 days, then take 12 pints of water and in it put 3 pounds of sugar to clarify with 3 egg whites. Let it boil ¾ hour. Pour out let stand 'til cold, strain parings. Add juice 4 oranges or 6 lemons. Keep close stop't for 6 weeks. Draw off.

A 19th CENTURY PUNCH

In a 19th century cook book, the use of beer was described as "a good family drink. The winter wintergreen, thrown in, is very beneficial to humors."

1 quart white wine	*1 pint lemon soda*
3 jiggers sherry wine	*Dash Bitters*
2 jiggers brandy	*Sugar to taste*
½ cup ale or beer	*Juice 1 lemon*

Mix all ingredients together, taste for sweetness. Add more sugar if needed.

A LEMON DRINK

19th century

"More refreshing than a dipper of water."

This receipt was frequently found in the older cookbooks and was described as a good drink for the farmer's wife to carry out to the men in the field on a hot day.

4 lemons	*1 compressed yeast cake*
4 pounds sugar	*1 slice nut-brown toast*
4 oz. ground ginger root	

Peel the lemons thinly, and cut into thin slices. Mix the sugar and ginger root together. Add to the lemon slices. Let stand for a few hours. Add the water and let stand until cool. Set the yeast on the toast and float on the surface. Let stand from 4 to 6 hours, stirring frequently, remove the toast, and strain the liquid into sterilized bottles. Cork tightly and lay the bottles on their side for 12 hours. Store in a cool place.

MULLED GRAPE JUICE

1880

1 quart grape juice
1 pint boiling water
1 cup sugar
1 dozen cloves

One 2-inch stick cinnamon
Thin rind and juice 2
lemons

Stir sugar in boiling water until sugar is dissolved.
Combine grape juice, water and sugar in enamel saucepan. Tie spices in a small cheesecloth bag, tie loosely. Add the spice bag to the mixture and simmer over low heat just to boiling point. Remove spice bag. Add the rind and juice. Remove from heat, stir well and let stand for 10 to 15 minutes. Serve in heated mugs.

PUNCHEON PUNCH

The word "Punch" is said to derive from the ancient word "Puncheon" which was the original name of the casks in which wine was aged.

*2-quart block of Lemon Water
Ice (available at markets)
4 quarts Chablis or 2 quarts
each Club soda and Chablis*

*Or: ½ Champagne and
½ Chablis or Sauterne
Thinly sliced lemons*

Chill punch bowl with ice cubes. Discard before adding block of water ice. Drop an ice cube in each punch glass. At serving time, place the block of water ice in chilled bowl. Pour the selected liquids over and stir well. As the water ice melts, the ladle will pick up small portions of it to add to the punch glasses. Garnish the punch bowl with the lemon slices. Discard the ice cube in each glass before serving each guest. Do not fill a quantity of glasses ahead of time.

FRONT PORCH PUNCH

*1 pint water
Juice 3 lemons
Juice 6 oranges
1 cup currant juice*

*1 cup strong tea
2-inch stick cinnamon
Club soda
Orange slices*

Combine water, lemon and orange juice. Refrigerate for several hours. Add currant juice, and the tea steeped for several minutes with the cinnamon. Chill before adding to punch.

Current Juice

Wash one quart red currants in cold water. Strip from stems, crush with ½ cup sugar and simmer slowly over low heat until currants turn white. Press through fine wire sieve or pour into a flannel jelly bag and hang from a nail over a large bowl.

Partially fill tall glasses with chopped ice, add punch and fill glasses with club soda. Garnish glasses with thin slices of orange.

FRUIT PUNCH

2 quarts grape juice	*2 quarts ginger ale*
Juice 1 dozen oranges	*1 pint Simple Syrup (p. 224)*
Juice 1 dozen lemons	*1 pint strong tea*

Combine all ingredients with exception of ginger ale and club soda. Chill the punch, then pour into chilled punch bowl over a block of ice. When ready to serve, add the ale and/or the soda. Garnish with thin slices of orange and lemon.

PARTY PUNCH

Juice 12 lemons	*2 quarts cider*
Grated rind 2 lemons	*1 quart club soda*
Juice 4 oranges	*1 quart sliced strawberries*
Grated rind 2 oranges	*Maraschino cherries, and thin*
2 pounds sugar (or less)	*sliced lemon and orange for*
1 quart strong, fresh tea	*garnish*

Combine lemon juice, rind, orange juice and rind with the sugar and the chilled tea. Stir well, cover and let stand for a few hours in refrigerator. When ready to serve, pour over a block of ice in punch bowl, add cider and club soda. Taste, and if more sweetening is needed, add a little simple syrup (p. 224). Garnish and serve in punch glasses. Should be very, very cold. Add a spoonful of the strawberries to each punch glass.

FEBRUARY PARTY PUNCH

A two–quart block Red Rasp-
berry Water Ice (see p. 159)
1 quart bottled cranberry juice

1 quart light ginger ale
2 quarts club soda

Chill the punch bowl well. Drop an ice cube in each punch glass. (Read the Puncheon Punch directions p. 195). Proceed as described.

STRAWBERRY PUNCH

(In season)

2 quarts fresh strawberries
1 cup sugar
Juice 3 lemons

Juice 6 oranges
Club soda

Wash strawberries,* hull and cover with the sugar. Simmer over low heat for a few minutes. Press through a fine sieve or blender. Cool and add fruit juice. Chill for several hours. Pour into tall glasses, partially filled with chopped ice. Fill with club soda. Decorate each with a fresh berry.

* The proper way to wash berries is as follows:
Fill a bowl with tepid water and fill a second bowl with cold water. Let the berries stand in the tepid water for a brief minute. Lift out with hands or slotted spoon. Do not pour out. Drop into cold water. Lift out and dry on paper towel. Hull berries when ready to use. The dry, unhulled berries may be tightly covered and kept in refrigerator for a few hours, or frozen for 2 to 3 months.

TEA

The story of tea begins, as do many of our basic foods, with a delightful, purely apocryphal Chinese legend, which runs as follows: "In the year 2737 B.C. leaves from a wild tea bush fell by chance into the Emperor Shen Nung's boiling drinking water. 'What a delightful flavor,' said the wise Emperor, drinking the world's first cup of tea."

The story of tea then jumps to 780 A.D. when the Chinese poet, Lu-Yu, published the first book about tea. And from then on, tea bushes were grown in China and Japan. By the seventeenth century, the East India Company began to bring tea to England from Java. They were perilous journeys and many ships were sunk by pirates and cutthroats and by storms. A few brave men decided to try another method of transportation: by camel caravan from China across the deserts and mountains to Eastern Europe, a journey of eighteen months.

By the midseventeenth century, tea was well established as a popular beverage, even though it sold at the equivalent of about ten dollars a pound in today's currency. The housewife served it in delicate porcelain cups as a very weak brew, with no milk.

By the eighteenth century, it was England's national beverage, and by the nineteenth century tea bushes were found growing wild in northeast India. Today Indonesia is the largest grower of tea.

Emigrants to the New World carried large supplies of tea, as did their descendants who made the journey by covered wagon to open up new territory in the West. Today the United States is the second largest user of tea in the whole world.

The growing, cultivation, plucking and processing of the tea leaves is an extremely complex and tedious task. When ready to be shipped, the cargoes of tea are packed in moisture-proof chests, light and easy to handle. The cargoes travel by tramp steamer and ocean liner to every port in the world, where they are finally delivered to tea companies, who perform the delicate task of blending. This is the skilled work of the tea tasters. And as there are over 3000 varieties of teas from which to choose, the task is tremendous. Like wines, teas take their names from the districts where they were grown.

The tea today's shopper buys is a blend of 20 to 30 different varieties, each chosen for a certain characteristic color, flavor, bouquet, body. The confusion in the shopper's mind arises when she is faced with three different titles: black, green and oolong. But every type comes from the same tea bush. The difference comes in the processing *after* the leaves are picked.

We Americans prefer black tea, which is fully fermented. Green tea is not fermented at all. Oolong tea is a compromise between the black and green. It is semifermented.

When made properly, tea is a delicious beverage—hot or iced, spiced or as an ingredient in a punch.

A "Proper" Cup of Tea

For the most perfect cup of hot tea, follow these directions:
Bring water (from the cold water faucet, never from the hot
water faucet) to a full rolling boil. Warm two *china* teapots.
Discard the hot water when the teapots are warmed.

For every cup of tea, allow one level teaspoon of tea to one
cup of the freshly boiling water. For a weaker cup of tea,
increase the water. Cover the teapot and let stand to steep
for three minutes.

Stir the tea and pour through a fine strainer into the
second warmed pot. Serve at once.

Never use a silver teapot to make the tea.

When serving a group of people, keep the teapot warm by
covering with an English Tea Cozy.

How To Make Good Iced Tea

Brew the tea exactly as you brew hot tea, but allow 50 percent more tea leaves to allow for melting ice. In other words,
if you use 4 teaspoons of tea leaves for a pot of hot tea, use
6 teaspoons for the same amount of water.

Many a good glass of ice tea is made flavorful with a stick
of cinnamon or a few cloves pierced in sliced lemons added
to the hot tea.

COFFEE

The great Brillat-Savarin wrote many aphorisms, one very
pertinent to today's housewives. "The mistress of the household must always make sure her coffee is excellent."

The history of coffee, oddly enough, is totally lacking in

mythical tales of shepherds, emperors and princes. But, on the other hand, it is replete with true tales of intrigue, hooded men and even a kidnaping—that of a plant, not a person. But like its peers, tea, sugar and chocolate, coffee has an ancient and interesting history.

The saga of coffee really began in Arabia, where reliable medical tomes printed in 900 A.D. mention its use. But it soon became a beverage that was drunk for pleasure, not as a dose of medicine. And as was the case with the production of the cacao bean, the secret of cultivation of the coffee bean was a jealously guarded secret for generations. Its struggle, too, for secrecy, was a long and losing one. By the year 1690 the enterprising Dutch succeeded in getting plants out of Arabia and into the botanical gardens in Holland.

The Dutch then began cultivation in Java and by the year 1706 Javanese coffee arrived in Amsterdam. Now the Dutch sent coffee plants all over Europe so that botanical gardens everywhere could experiment.

By the time of Louis XV, young coffee plants were flourishing in the Jardin des Plantes in Paris. And now the real intrigue to obtain the coffee plants began. A young French officer of Martinique headed a stealthy group of hooded men who stole a young coffee plant from the Royal Gardens.

In the spring of 1723 the young officer and his plant embarked for Martinique. The voyage was marked by disastrous storms, a water shortage and an attempted kidnaping by a conniving Dutchman. But fortunately the plant survived and showed extraordinary growth and development. Soon its progeny dotted the entire West Indies and eventually spread to the mainland of South America.

As the coffee production was such a valuable business asset, two small colonies, Dutch and French Guiana, became embroiled in a dispute and asked Brazil to send an emissary to settle the matter. This Brazil was delighted to do and sent a clever and skillful man who settled the dispute. Fortunately he was also a "Ladies' Man," and consequently went back home with a gift of fertile coffee beans and cuttings, concealed in a bouquet.

In the thousand years since it made its first recorded appearance, coffee has undergone many changes. It has been seasoned with spices, laced with liquors, blended with champagne and, in the twentieth century, blended with cream and whiskey, ignited and called Irish Coffee. At one time during its thousand-year era, street vendors sold coffee in tiny cups to strolling customers on the streets of Damascus and Cairo; thence, the custom was carried over to European cities and London. And it was the street vendors in London who preceded the establishment of the famous coffee houses of London.

In the seventeenth and eighteenth centuries, the coffee houses took their place with the newly sprung up chocolate houses and served as the daily newspapers of the times. Thus the congregation of witty and able men who gathered there daily played an important part in the political and literary life of the era.

In the classic *Pepys' Diary*, the writer mentions all three of the new beverages. Of coffee he writes, "I just looked in, on my way home from Covent Garden, at the great coffee houses there, where I never was before . . . and all the wits of the town were assembled." Of tea Pepys' said, "And afterwards I did send for a cup of tee (a China drink) of which I had never drunk before, and went away." The diarist also liked chocolate, as he noted, "And there drank my morning draft in good chocollatte."

The English essayist Joseph Addison said of coffee houses in *The Spectator* (dated March 1, 1711–12), the famous literary journal founded by Richard Steele: "The chief places of resort were coffee and chocolate houses, in which some men almost lived, insomuch that whoever wished to find a gentleman commonly asked, not where he resided, but which coffee house he frequented?"

Following the establishment of the coffee houses in London and European cities, English and Dutch ships brought coffee to the colonies. Again, coffee vendors paved the way for introducing the new beverage. Oddly enough, the first licensed vendor was a woman, this in 1670. And the first coffee house in America opened in 1689.

Like the blending of tea, the blending of coffee is a great art. The experts in the coffee world define a coffee blend as: "A flavor harmony of various coffees chosen for specific qualities and combined so as to form a congenial whole." But in previous centuries, dating back to the sixteenth, coffee was a single brew. It took nearly three centuries to bring about the process of skillful blending. By the early 1800's improved roasting and brewing equipment began to place emphasis on a better flavor, of more subtlety.

But until the commercial patents and inventions improved the process, the housewives of the late eighteenth and early nineteenth century roasted coffee at home. By the late nineteenth century, home roasting was nearly at the end of its era, but grinding the coffee fresh every morning remained a housewife's task until vacuum-packed coffee and coffee ground to her order at the big markets did away with it.

The writers of the cookbooks in the eighteenth and nineteenth centuries speak at length about making a good cup of coffee. One writer says, "It is the simplest thing in the world to make a good cup of coffee . . . . Very few housekeepers roast their own coffee." Another one says "Do not roast too much at a time; grind at the time of using . . . To Brown Coffee—'Put coffee, after being nicely washed, in a baking tin, place in a slow oven until pretty well dried, then increase the heat very much, and as soon as it browns up stir up very often; seat yourself by the oven and close the door, and let it brown until you hear it crack, then stir again, and do so until dark brown. Do not leave it after it begins to brown until taken out of the oven.' "

How To Make A "Decent" Cup of Coffee

The same rules for making a cup of tea apply to making a good cup of coffee. 1. Let the water run from the cold water faucet. 2. Bring the water to a full rolling boil. 3. Measure the coffee and the water accurately. 4. Be sure the coffee pot is immaculately clean. 5. A true coffee lover believes that coffee should be made by the drip method, in glass or china, never in metal. 6. Always scald the coffee maker before pouring in the boiling water. 7. The accepted measurements that the devoted coffee drinker prefers is two level table-spoons (or the coffee measure) to every ¾ cup of freshly boiling water. 8. Ultracritical coffee drinkers believe that the coffee container should be stored in the refrigerator year 'round.

CHOCOLATE

Chocolate is hailed the world over as the most popular of all flavors for cakes, pies, puddings, ice creams, candies, sauces and beverages. Yet it was not always so.

Returning from his voyage to the New World, Columbus laid a few, dark brown beans before the throne of Ferdinand, who was not at all impressed. It remained for the great Spanish explorer of the sixteenth century, Hernando Cortez, to grasp the commercial possibilities of the cacao bean. Cortez, following his conquest of Mexico, was royally entertained by the Emperor of the Aztecs, Montezuma. Chocolate was served to the invaders in golden goblets: cold, bitter and as thick as honey.

But the shrewd Spaniards observed the Aztec methods of cultivating and growing the cacao bean; liking very sweet foods, Cortez conceived the idea of adding cane sugar which was also making its bow on the culinary scene in Europe.

The Spanish people developed a profitable business and somehow managed to keep the art of cultivating the cacao bean a commercial secret for the next one hundred years.

But as Spain declined in power, the secret of the cacao bean industry became known all over Europe and England.

Soon the custom of drinking chocolate became fashionable all through the royal courts and among the very wealthy. By the midseventeenth century, wealthy Londoners flocked to Chocolate Houses and Clubs. But chocolate remained a rich man's delicacy and was consumed only as a beverage.

By the eighteenth century, the demand for the drink was so great that the small hand-methods of grinding the cacao beans were outstripped. And when steam and water power developed, chocolate was made by mass production methods.

In common with the other products of the day, (flour, coffee, sugar, tea), the demand and the new methods of manufacture brought the price down to such a degree that by the middle of the century, the moderately well-to-do middle class could afford the new product.

At the beginning of the nineteenth century, chocolate took on a new aspect. Cocoa powder was introduced and by the middle of the century eating chocolate was developed.

By the year 1876 Daniel Peter, the great Swiss, had manufactured the first milk chocolate. This new specialty was accompanied by the second development in chocolate manufacture: smooth, velvety chocolate pressed into firm half-pound blocks.

This fondant chocolate, as it was first called, replaced once and for all the old, coarse-grained chunky blocks of chocolate. This development is reflected in the difference between the receipts in the old cookbooks on both sides of the Atlantic and today's recipes. Directions invariably used to read, "Grate the chocolate." In this volume, directions for grated chocolate appear in but a few recipes, since melting the chocolate just about replaces grating.

Today's shoppers are confronted by every variety of chocolate: cocoa powder, milk chocolate, unsweetened chocolate, semi-sweet chocolate, in bars, in morsels and in tubes.

HOT CHOCOLATE

1 quart of milk	*¼ cup sugar*
2 to 4 squares unsweetened chocolate	*2 tablespoons boiling water*
⅛ teaspoon salt	*1 teaspoon vanilla extract**

Scald the milk over hot (not boiling) water. Mix the chocolate, salt, sugar and water in a small saucepan. Stir over low heat until the chocolate melts and the mixture is smooth and glossy. Pour a little of the hot milk over, return to heat and beat with a wire whisk to form a frothy texture. Pour into a heated china pot and serve immediately with a bowl of sweetened whipped cream.

The four squares of chocolate make a very rich beverage. Do not allow the beverage to stand after it is finished.

* For afternoon chocolate, the addition of the flavoring is very good.

HOT CHOCOLATE II

1 (6 oz.) package semi-sweet
  chocolate or 6 squares semi-
  sweet chocolate (6 oz.)
1 cup water

⅛ teaspoon salt
1 pint whipping cream
1-to-2 cups milk

Combine the chocolate, salt and water. Stir over low heat until it forms a smooth paste. Scald the milk and cream over hot water. Add a little of the hot liquid to the chocolate mixture, return to heat and beat with a wire whisk until frothy and light. Serve in heated teacups. Garnish with sweetened whipped cream.

HOT COCOA

1 quart of milk
¼ cup Breakfast Cocoa
¼ cup cold water

2 to 4 tablespoons sugar
⅛ teaspoon salt

Scald the milk over hot (not boiling) water. Mix the cocoa with the water, salt and sugar to make a smooth paste. Add a little of the hot milk to the mixture, stir well and return to the heat. Simmer for just one minute, beating with a wire whisk.
Serve in heated teacups.

Herbs, Spices
and Wine in Cookery

The pages of the history books abound with tales of high adventure on the seven seas, of the search for rare herbs and spices to be found on the famous spice islands. But the adventure and romance no longer exist. Fleets of fast ships and planes have replaced the old "wooden ships and iron men" in the interest of efficiency.

In casual mention, herbs and spices are used interchangeably. But to be botanically correct, they are defined in the *Standard Encyclopedia of Horticulture* as follows: "Herbs are always leaves of plants that grow in temperate zones; seeds, such as mustard, caraway, and poppy are actually seeds, or sometimes the fruit of plants that grow in temperate or tropical zones. True spices are parts of plants that usually grow in the tropics. And quite contrary to popular opinion, spices are seldom 'hot' in flavor, but are quite mild."

To specify still further: Ginger is the rootstock of the plant; cinnamon is the inner bark of the plant; clove is the flowerbud of the plant; nutmeg is the seed of the plant. Allspice received its popular name because it was thought to have the flavor of cinnamon, nutmeg and cloves.

In the days of old, spices were scarce, expensive and hard

to come by; as a consequence they were held in high esteem. Today, spices are in every kitchen, and are accepted as an everyday condiment. Their use in desserts is as great as in early centuries, so much so, in fact, that at the end of the nineteenth century, over 200,000,000 pounds of spices a year were consumed in the United States alone.

In this cookbook, there is frequent mention of spices used in breads, cakes, puddings and sundry dishes. The most popular spices used in these dishes include allspice, caraway seed, cinnamon, clove, ginger, nutmeg.

Cooking with herbs requires no special recipes nor unusual methods. It is well to note, however, that the herb seasoning should be done with a light hand, and that not more than two dishes at one meal should include herb seasoning.

Buy your supply of herbs and spices in the smallest possible sizes. Dried herbs lose their fragrance within a few months' time. Keep them away from heat and direct sunlight.

Herbs with which to start your herb shelf might include bay leaves, marjoran or oregano, thyme, dill seed, paprika. For the spice shelf include stick cinnamon, ground cinnamon, cloves, whole cloves, nutmeg, allspice and any of the others that are used frequently. But don't overstock your shelves.

COOKING WITH WINE

Our forebears knew the use of wine and ale, or beer, in cookery.

The use of ale or beer today in cooking serves several desirable functions. It tenderizes an inexpensive cut of meat.

It adds flavor to a meat or cheese dish. It provides additional zest in dried fruit desserts, such as compotes. And it is economical to use, since part of an opened bottle may be used.

The addition of wine to cooked food or to food to be cooked is an old, old technique—one that deserves to be employed in modern kitchens. The characteristic differences in the flavor and color of the different varieties of dessert wines give the cook great scope in preparing delicious desserts.

The one point to remember is the same as in using fresh eggs, butter, and other food ingredients. The quality of the dish will be the same as the quality of the wine. A poor, thin or sour wine will lend the same flavor to the finished dish. However a partially opened bottle is as satisfactory as an unused bottle. And an expensive wine is not at all necessary.

There are many famous desserts which have come down to the twentieth century from the past. Probably the most popular and well-known one is Crêpes Suzette. Like similar recipes, this one has an anecdote associated with it.

It seems that Napoleon Bonaparte, during the harsh winter of the war with Russia, was delighted with a new dish which his chef served. So he asked him what the special thin pancakes, soaked in brandy, were called. "Crêpes Suzette, Your Majesty." "And who is Madam Suzette"?

"My wife, Your Majesty. And I miss her so much."

According to the tale, it seems that food was very scarce and the meals monotonous, so the ingenious chef created the first Crepes Suzette.

As is the case in beer cookery, the alcohol in wine steams away at 40° F. long before water boils at 212° F. but the flavor remains to add zest to the dish. The food should be warm when the wine is added (cooked food) and the wine also must be warm if it is to be ignited.

APPLE PUDDING WITH PORT

Preheat oven to 375°.   *8 x 8 x 2-inch pan*

4 tart cooking apples   1 tablespoon lemon juice
½ cup claret or port wine

Core, peel and cut the apples in thin slices, sprinkle with lemon juice and cover with the wine. Cover bowl and let stand.
Prepare the topping as follows:

Topping

¼ cup sifted all-purpose flour   ½ teaspoon cinnamon
1 cup brown sugar, firmly   ½ teaspoon nutmeg
  packed   ¼ cup melted butter

Mix all ingredients together. Butter the baking dish, arrange the sliced apples, pour the liquid over and spread the topping over the mixture. Bake until the apples are tender. Serve warm with Foamy Sauce (p. 221).

A PERFECT BANANA DESSERT

Preheat oven to 350°.   *Oblong baking dish*

3 ripe bananas   3 tablespoons melted butter
  (but not dead ripe)   3 tablespoons brown sugar
12 fingers of bread   3 tablespoons sherry wine
12 spoonfuls of jam   1 tablespoon lemon juice
1 tablespoon lemon juice

Peel the bananas and cut in half lengthwise and then in half crosswise. Cut the bread in finger shape to place under each banana portion. Butter the bread, and spread with jam. Place each banana piece on top, press down lightly and sprinkle with lemon juice. Combine the butter, sugar and wine and spread over the top. Bake until sugar is soft and bubbly. Serve hot, with cream or ice cream.

FRESH FRUITS IN WINE

Many a dessert may be prepared, using wine as the center of interest. A combination of two fruits or even three is very attractive. Do not "drown" the fruits in the wine. Pour just enough of the wine over the fruit to lend its bouquet. Fresh pineapple, cut into chunks, and stirred gently with strawberries is a good combination with *rosé* wine.

Fresh red raspberries and melon balls with a sweet Sauterne is also good.

Use any fresh fruit in season or a good quality of canned fruit, such as peach or pear halves.

PEACHES IN SAUTERNE WINE

6 fresh peaches *or*
12 canned peach halves
Wine glass of sauterne

2 tablespoons unsalted butter
½ cup sugar
⅛ teaspoon salt

Peel the peaches, cut in half, and pour the wine over. Let stand for one or more hours. In a small skillet, bring the butter to the foaming point, carefully heat the peach halves on both sides. Lift out with slotted spoon, place in shallow dessert dish. Combine the wine, sugar, salt and butter in the skillet and simmer over low heat until syrupy. Pour over the peaches and chill well before serving. Serve with a soft custard or with cream. May also be served hot. Peach stones need not be removed. They add a bit of extra flavor.

When the peaches are served hot, a small quantity of brandy is ignited and poured over the hot syrup, spooning it up until the flames die down. The brandy must be heated in order to ignite.

PEARS POACHED IN WINE

4 fresh Bartlett pears, not quite ripe	⅛ teaspoon salt
½ cup sugar	Thin peel of 1 lemon, cut in strips
½ cup strained honey	½ cup sherry or muscatel

Cut pears in half lengthwise. Scoop out the core with a spoon. Set aside. Combine all ingredients and simmer over low heat for 15 minutes. Add the pears (unpeeled) and simmer for 5 minutes. Remove peel. Let stand until cool, transfer to pretty serving dish. Cover and chill for several hours. Serve with custard sauce (p. 225).

SAUTERNE WINE JELLY

2 tablespoons gelatin	⅛ teaspoon salt
½ cup cold water	1 cup (about) sugar
1¼ cups boiling water	¼ cup freshly squeezed lemon juice
2 cups Sauterne wine	
Few drops green food coloring	

Sprinkle the gelatin over the cold water; let stand to soften. Pour boiling water over and stir until gelatin is dissolved. Add the remaining ingredients and stir. Taste to see if more sugar is needed. This is a very pretty jelly. Serve it in tall glasses, decorated with green maraschino cherries and/or sweetened whipped cream.

WINE POTPOURRI

1 pound dried fruits (apricots, prunes, raisins)
½ to ¾ cup sugar

Claret wine to cover
One 2-inch stick cinnamon
Thin strips of lemon peel

Rinse the fruits in cold water. Cover with the claret wine and soak for 12 hours. Add the sugar, spice and peel. Simmer over low heat until the fruit is very soft, but not mushy. Lift out fruit, spice and peel with a slotted spoon and discard spice and peel. Cook the syrup down to a thick syrupy consistency. Cool and pour over the fruit. Chill thoroughly and serve with cream.

This dessert is also very good prepared with a bottle of ale. A partially opened bottle of ale or wine is suitable for this dessert.

For an additional spicy flavor add a few whole cloves. If whole cloves are used, it is advisable to tie cloves and cinnamon loosely in a small cheesecloth bag.

Extra large, fancy whole prunes are very good prepared in this manner.

ZABAGLIONE

This is probably the best known of all wine desserts and it is delicious, either hot or cold.

6 egg yolks
6 tablespoons sugar

6 tablespoons sweet sherry or
muscatel

Combine the three ingredients, place in saucepan over hot (not boiling) water. The water must *not* boil or the mixture will be ruined.

Beat with a rotary egg beater until the mixture is very fluffy. Pour into glass dessert dishes and either serve at once, or allow to stand until well chilled.

Dessert Sauces

The art of making a perfect sauce, well-seasoned, perfectly blended, smooth and velvety, has always been held in high regard by gourmets, chefs de cuisine and any lover of a good dinner. In the days of the great chefs, in the seventeenth century, when the sauces were very superior, the chef was given a special title to portray his importance. He was respected as the Saucier.

Prior to the seventeenth century, the combinations of foods were often strange and peculiar. A delightful little treatise, with the intriguing title, *The Young Cook's Monitor*, (1683) had this to say: "Some of the ingredients proposed for Sauces seem to our ears to be rather prodigious."

However, as the elaborate and time-consuming sauce-making fell into disfavor, some of the substitutes were about as bad from the viewpoint of the gourmet. But, again, the pendulum is swinging back to good sauces, but simpler and delicious.

For a good sauce is the crowning touch to a fine dessert.

BRANDY SAUCE

½ cup unsalted butter
1 to 2 cups 10-X sugar

1 egg, well beaten
Brandy to taste

Cream butter; add the sugar gradually. Add the egg and beat well. Add the brandy gradually until taste suits palate. Serve with a steamed pudding.
Egg may be omitted.

BUTTERSCOTCH SAUCE

½ cup unsalted butter
½ pint whipping cream
1 pound light brown sugar

⅛ teaspoon salt
¼ cup white corn syrup*

Combine all ingredients in upper part of double boiler over hot, not boiling, water. Stir frequently until the sugar and butter are dissolved. Cover and simmer over low heat two to three hours, stirring occasionally.
Cool and pour into glass jars. Cover and refrigerate. Will keep well for several weeks. When ready to serve, pour amount needed in saucepan and reheat over hot (not boiling) water.

*For a more caramelly consistency, increase the amount of corn syrup to ½ cup.

CHERRY SAUCE

1 (No. 2) can sour pitted
    cherries
Cold water

1 cup sugar
2 tablespoons cornstarch
⅛ teaspoon salt

Drain the cherries, measure the juice and add enough of the cold water to measure 1 cupful of liquid. Combine the sugar, cornstarch and salt. Stir together well. Add the cupful of liquid. Simmer over low heat until smooth and slightly thickened. Add the drained cherries and serve warm over a Blanc Mange or a plain pudding.

CHOCOLATE SAUCE

4 squares unsweetened chocolate	½ cup white corn syrup
	⅛ teaspoon salt
½ cup water	1 teaspoon vanilla extract
1 cup sugar	2 tablespoons butter

Melt chocolate and water together over hot (not boiling) water. Add the remaining ingredients, with the exception of flavoring and butter.
Stir the mixture frequently until the sugar is dissolved. Cover and simmer for 1 hour or longer. Stir occasionally. Pour into glass jar, cover and refrigerate. Keeps well. When ready to serve, reheat the amount needed.

CHOCOLATE SAUCE II

1 (one pound) package milk chocolate	¼ cup hot water
	½ pint whipping cream
⅛ teaspoon salt	1 teaspoon vanilla extract

Break the chocolate into pieces, melt over hot (not boiling) water. Add the salt and water, stir lightly and set aside to cool. Whip the cream and add the chocolate slowly, gently stirring constantly. Add the flavoring and serve either as a dessert in parfait glasses or as a sauce over ice cream.

CHOCOLATE SAUCE III

1 cup sugar
½ cup light cream
¼ to ½ cup white corn syrup
3 squares unsweetened chocolate

3 tablespoons water
⅛ teaspoon salt
1 teaspoon vanilla extract

Combine the sugar, cream and corn syrup. Bring just to boiling point over direct heat, stirring constantly. In a separate saucepan, over hot (not boiling) water, melt the chocolate and add the water. Let cool slightly and add to the sugar mixture. Stir together, add the salt and flavoring. Keep hot over hot water. Serve while hot over ice cream.

CREAM SAUCE

½ pint light cream
2 tablespoons butter
1 tablespoon flour
1 cup 10-X sugar

⅛ teaspoon salt
¼ to ½ pint white wine
½ teaspoon nutmeg

Simmer the cream, just to the boiling point. Remove from heat and cool slightly. Rub butter and flour together (called a roux) and add sugar. Beat well. Add the cream slowly, beating constantly. Add the salt and set aside to chill. Beat in the wine to taste. Sprinkle with the nutmeg.

ENGLISH SWEET SAUCE

1 tablespoon cornstarch
½ cup sugar
⅛ teaspoon salt
¼ cup cold milk

1 cup scalded milk
1 egg yolk
1 teaspoon vanilla extract

Stir dry ingredients together and blend with cold milk to make a smooth paste. Add the hot milk gradually and stir until smooth. Return to saucepan, over hot water, and cook until slightly thickened. Add egg yolk and beat quickly. Add the flavoring and serve hot over a warm pudding.

A GOOD SAUCE FOR FRENCH TOAST

1856

1 cup unsalted butter
1 pound 10-X sugar
6 egg yolks
2 egg whites

Grated rind 2 lemons
Juice of 3 lemons (dry lemons
　　in sun for 3 days)

Cream butter and sugar together until well blended. Beat egg yolks until thick and lemon colored and add to butter, sugar mixture. Add grated rind and lemon juice; beat well. Whip whites to stiff peaks and fold into the mixture. Heap high on hot fresh French Toast.

A GOOD PUDDING SAUCE

1888

½ cup butter
1 cup light brown sugar
1 cup whipping cream

Hot water for thinning
2 tablespoons good brandy*

Combine butter, sugar and cream. Stir over low heat until sugar is dissolved. Add enough hot water for desired consistency. Simmer for 5 minutes. Add brandy and serve at once.

* The early writers always specified that the brandy and wines used in cooking must be "good quality."

TRADITIONAL HARD SAUCE

1 cup unsalted butter
2 to 3 cups 10-X sugar

⅛ teaspoon salt
Brandy to taste

Cream butter; add the sugar gradually. Add the salt and stir in the brandy alternately with the sugar until the consistency is thick and creamy. Pack in bowl, cover tightly and refrigerate. Keeps indefinitely.

Foamy Sauce

Hard sauce
1 egg, well beaten
⅛ teaspoon salt

Heat the hard sauce in a saucepan over hot (not boiling) water. As soon as it softens, beat in the egg and salt. Stirring constantly, beat the egg into the sauce and continue to beat until the mixture is soft and foamy. Serve at once. Does not keep well.

HOT SAUCE FOR STEAMED PUDDING

1 cup unsalted butter
1½ cups light brown sugar, firmly packed
½ teaspoon nutmeg

⅛ teaspoon salt
½ cup brandy, heated
(do not add a cold liquid to a hot mixture)

Combine butter, sugar and salt. Simmer over low heat until syrupy. Add the nutmeg and add the brandy gradually to suit taste. Let come to boil, remove from heat and serve warm.

Variation

2 egg yolks, well beaten. Pour a little of the hot sauce over the yolks and stir in just before removing from heat. Strain through wire sieve.

A DELICATE LEMON SAUCE

2 whole lemons
1 cup sugar
½ cup butter, softened

1 tablespoon flour
1 cup boiling water
Pinch of nutmeg

Scrub lemons well with stiff-bristled brush. Cover with cold water, bring to boil and simmer over low heat until a skewer penetrates skin easily. Cool and cut into very thin slices. Set aside. Discard water.

Stir together sugar, butter and flour in saucepan. Add boiling water slowly, stirring constantly, until sauce is smooth and free from lumps. Strain and add lemon slices, dust with nutmeg. Serve over hot puddings.

MADEIRA SAUCE

(*Monsieur Gouffé*)

8 egg yolks	Grated rind ½ lemon
½ cup sugar	1½ cups Madeira wine

Beat egg yolks until thick, add sugar gradually. Simmer over hot (not boiling) water, stirring constantly, adding the wine slowly and carefully. As soon as the sauce clings to the spoon, strain through a fine sieve and add the grated rind. Serve hot.

ORANGE SAUCE

2 egg yolks	1½ cups orange juice
½ cup sugar	Grated rind ½ lemon
⅛ teaspoon salt	3 tablespoons lemon juice
Grated rind 1 orange	

Beat egg yolks until very thick. Add the sugar gradually and beat until the mixture falls like a ribbon from the spoon. Add the salt, fruit juices and rinds. Simmer over hot (not boiling water) until thickened and smooth. Taste and, if necessary, add 1 teaspoon almond extract.

RED RASPBERRY SAUCE

For Lemon Souffle or Pêche Melba

1 pint red raspberries, fresh, frozen or canned	*2 to 4 tablespoons sugar*
2 tablespoons cornstarch	*⅛ teaspoon salt*
	2 tablespoons cold water

Simmer the berries over low heat until just at the boiling point, but do not allow to boil. If the berries are canned or frozen and therefore, sweetened, two tablespoons of sugar are enough. Combine the cornstarch with the sugar and salt. Mix with the cold water to make a smooth paste. Rub the berries through a fine sieve or through a blender and add the syrup to the sugar mixture. Return to heat and simmer for 3 to 5 minutes. Chill before serving. A tablespoon or two of brandy is a nice addition to this sauce.

A SIMPLE SAUCE

1 cup sugar
½ cup water
1 tablespoon cornstarch   } *Stir together to a smooth paste*
2 tablespoons cold water
¼ cup brandy or sherry

Simmer sugar and water together until syrupy. Pour over the cornstarch paste. Return to low heat and simmer until slightly thickened. Add the flavoring and serve hot. If necessary, strain through wire sieve.

PERFECT SOFT CUSTARD SAUCE

4 egg yolks, lightly beaten	1 cup light cream
½ cup sugar	1 cup milk
⅛ teaspoon salt	1 teaspoon vanilla extract

Combine the egg yolks, sugar and salt; stir until well blended. Scald milk and cream and add slowly to mixture, stirring constantly. Return to saucepan over hot (not boiling) water. Simmer until thickened (mixture will cling to spoon when the custard is the right consistency). It must be stirred constantly and removed from the heat at the right moment or it will start to curdle.

Add the flavoring. Sherry wine is a good substitute for the vanilla.

The consistency is better if the custard is strained before cooling. Stir occasionally while cooling.

THRIFTY VANILLA SAUCE

½ to ¾ cup sugar	½ teaspoon nutmeg
2 tablespoons cornstarch	1 teaspoon vanilla extract
1 pint boiling water	½ teaspoon lemon extract
⅛ teaspoon salt	

Combine sugar and cornstarch until well blended. Pour boiling water on all at once and stir rapidly. Simmer over low heat until slightly thickened. Add salt, nutmeg and flavoring. Stir in and serve warm. Or pour into sauce boat and sprinkle with the nutmeg.

A tablespoon or two of butter is a pleasing addition.

WHIPPED CREAM SAUCE

1 pint whipping cream
½ cup 10-X sugar
1 teaspoon almond extract

½ teaspoon vanilla extract
Red food coloring

Whip the cream just before serving. Slowly sift in the sugar and stir together lightly. Stir in the flavoring and add a few drops of the food coloring to tint the sauce a delicate pink. Serve over a plain pudding, or over a wine jelly.

If served with a Sauterne jelly, which has been tinted a delicate green, tint the cream the same tint.

WINE SAUCES

I

1 tablespoon flour
2 tablespoons sugar
1 tablespoon butter
⅛ teaspoon salt

1 cup boiling water
1 cup white wine
¼ teaspoon grated nutmeg

Combine flour and sugar, add butter and salt. Pour boiling water over all at once, stir briskly. Add wine, let come to boil. Remove from heat at once. Sprinkle with nutmeg and serve over hot pudding.

II

1½ cups sugar (powdered)
¼ pound butter
⅛ teaspoon salt

1 cup white wine
¼ teaspoon grated nutmeg

Cream butter and sugar together. Add salt and beat in wine until thin enough to pour. Sprinkle with nutmeg. Serve with steamed pudding.

III

1856

½ cup unsalted butter
1 cup confectioners sugar

Juice and grated rind 1 lemon
1 cup white wine

Cream butter and sugar together, beat in rind and lemon juice. Bring wine to boiling point. Remove from heat and slowly add to sauce, beating constantly. Serve over a hot pudding, such as fig or plum.

Preserves

The preservation of fresh fruit and berries has been known to generations of housewives, but the first record of marmalade dates back to the reign of Henry VII, when the original marmalade was prepared from fresh quinces. The name *marmelo* (quince) originated in Portugal.

Today the use of preserves is such a commonplace part of the diet that the correct terms have been interchanged carelessly. The accurate definitions of some of the more widely used preserves are as follows:

Conserves or preserves: fruit preserved with sugar, the style and purpose varying with the user of the term. Conserve is usually considered a synonym for preserves.

Chutney: originally an Indian delicacy, prepared from mangoes, chillies, spices, peaches, raisins, lemons, ginger. There are two varieties: sweet and sour. Chutney is also the name given to any preserve which contains a mixture of ingredients, such as raisins, nut meats and fresh fruit, cooked together with sugar until very thick.

Jams: cooked fruits and/or berries or fruit pulps.

Jelly: cooked fruit juices, with the fibrous part of the pulp removed.

Marmalade: a semi-liquid preserve; typically of thick-rind, acid or bitter fruits, such as Seville or bitter oranges, grapefruit, (or sweet oranges and lemons), made by boiling the pulp or the juice with portions of the rind. Of all the varieties of marmalade, the Orange Marmalade, made from the Seville oranges is by far the most popular. Quince marmalade runs it a close second, if the quinces used are the "apple-quince" the choicest variety of quince. Quinces are also stewed with apples, sweetened with sugar and served as a sauce.

Glacé Fruit: a synonym for Candied Fruit.

Candied Fruit: also described as Crystallized Fruit. The fruit is boiled in sugar to the saturation point. The cooking is repeated many times, with a heavier syrup used each time. At the final cooking, corn syrup is added which gives a tender, satiny finish or glaze. Hence the name, glacéed fruit. This treatment is used for cherries, pineapple, citron.

17th CENTURY CONSERVES

"To make conserve of any fruit you please, you shall take the fruit, and if it be stone fruit, you shall take out the stones; if other fruit, take away the paring and core, and then boyl them in fair running water to a reasonable height, then drain them from thence, and put them into a fresh vessel with Claret-Wine or White-wine, according to the colour of the fruit; and so boyl them to a thick pap, all to mashing, breaking and stirring them together; and then to every pound of pap, put to a pound of Sugar, and so stirre them all well together; and straine them, and so pot it up."

Aside from the ancient spelling, this receipt is unchanged from many recipes in use today.

These preserves are so luscious that the modern housewife will find it well worthwhile to bring the receipt back into favor. They are superb as an ice cream topping.

WHOLE CRAB APPLES

These are a very popular delicacy.

Whole ripe crab apples   *Sugar*

Allow one pound of sugar (minus 2 tablespoons) to every pound of the apples. The crab apples must be ripe, but free from blemish or soft spots. The stems may be left on. Parboil the crab apples in boiling water for 5 minutes. Lift out with slotted spoon. Measure the sugar, allowing ½ pint of water to every pound. Simmer over low heat, stirring constantly until sugar is dissolved. Add the crab apples. If the skin is very hard, prick the skin with a long needle.
Simmer until the apples are tender, but hold their shape. Pour into hot sterilized jars. Cover tightly.

CURRANT JELLY—UNCOOKED

Fresh red currants   *Sugar*

Allow one pound of currants (stemmed) to each pound of sugar. Wash the currants well, drain and pull the currants from their stems. Weigh the currants. Squeeze them through a flannel jelly bag. Suspend the bag from a low hook and squeeze the juice into a large bowl. Pour the weighed sugar into a separate bowl and very, very slowly pour the juice over the sugar, stirring constantly until it jellies. Pour into sterilized *cold* jelly glasses. Cover with rounds of paper soaked in brandy and tie down tightly.

ORANGE MARMALADE

Navel oranges   *Sugar, pound for pound*

Wash the oranges, wipe dry and peel carefully. Cut from top to base, in quarters. Cover the peel with cold water, simmer for 1½ to 2 hours, or until the peel is very tender. (Test with a long-handled skewer.) Slice the oranges crosswise and sprinkle with the sugar. Drain the peel, cool and scrape out the inner white peel or pith. Now, slice the peel into the finest of thin shreds; the finer it is, the more attractive the marmalade.

Combine the sugared oranges, peel and stir well. Simmer over very low heat until thick and jellied. Pour into hot, sterilized jars. Cover tightly.

If it is possible to purchase Seville oranges, these are preferable, but they are difficult to find in the markets.

ORANGES—PRESERVED WHOLE

This is a bit of trouble, but the results are so satisfactory it is worth the time and effort.

Whole navel oranges   *Sugar, pound for pound*
The sugar and oranges must be weighed accurately.

Wipe the oranges with a damp cloth. Dry and grate on a

fine grater slightly. Do not over-grate. The skin must retain
its color.

Drop the oranges in a large kettle and simmer over low heat
until the rind is tender. Test with a long-handled skewer.
Let cool slightly, and drop into a boiling hot syrup of the
weighed sugar and water (equal quantity of sugar and
water). Simmer over low heat. The oranges will remain
whole and they are done when clear and transparent. They
may be cut in halves or in quarters and served as a garnish
for puddings or cold soufflés.

PEACH MARMALADE

Peaches   *Sugar*

To every pound of peaches, allow one-half pound sugar.
Peel peaches according to directions for pickled peaches
(p. 234). Slice very thin. In a large, wide-mouthed kettle,
arrange a layer of peach slices, cover with a layer of sugar
and continue until all peaches and sugar are used. Place
over very low heat, stirring constantly. The peaches are
cooked when they are clear and transparent.

Large Slices

Allow three-quarters of a pound of sugar to every pound of
peaches.

PEAR PRESERVES

6 pounds nearly ripe pears   2 quarts cold water
4½ pounds sugar

Wash the pears, peel, remove core and seeds. Slice pears into very thin slices. Pour into kettle, add the water and let come to a boil. Simmer until the pears are soft. Add the sugar and stir constantly. The mixture must be watched to prevent burning. When bubbles rise to the top, remove from heat and pour into hot, sterilized glasses. Thin slices of unpeeled lemon or a few pieces of candied ginger add a little zest to this mild marmalade. Cut the ginger into very small pieces.

PICKLED LEMONS

A dinner relish

1856

16 lemons
½ pound salt
1 gallon mild cider vinegar
Tie the following spices in a piece of clean cheesecloth:

¼ oz. each: whole cloves, grated nutmeg, mace, cayenne pepper, sliver of peeled garlic, 2 oz. mustard seed

Scrub lemons with stiff-bristled brush. Pour salt and vinegar into large *enamel* kettle. Bring to boil, add packet of spices and let simmer for 5 minutes. Add lemons and simmer until lemons are tender when pierced with skewer. Discard cheesecloth. Divide lemons into pint jars (sterilized and hot) and pour mixture over lemons. Seal tightly. Serve after ripening for a few weeks.

PICKLED PEACHES, PLUMS, CHERRIES

7 pounds of fruit
1 ounce ground cinnamon
1 ounce allspice
¼ ounce cloves (or whole cloves)

3 pounds sugar
1 quart pure cider vinegar

Wash the fruit well, prick the cherries and the plums with a long sharp needle. Peel the peaches.

Tie the spices in a small cheesecloth bag and tie loosely. The peaches may be pierced with the whole cloves. Combine the sugar, vinegar and spice bag; stir until the sugar is dissolved. Simmer over low heat until it comes to a boil. Skim it. Line a colander with a piece of clean, dampened cheesecloth. Remove the spice bag and pour the liquid into the colander, bring to a boil and pour over the fruit.

Let stand for 24 hours. Pour off the juice, bring to a boil and pour over the fruit again. Let stand 24 hours. Bring the fruit and syrup to a boil. When cold, pour into a stone crock, cover tightly and keep in a cool, dry place.

The Spice Bag

After the spice bag is removed, taste the syrup and if necessary, add the spices for the second boiling.

PICKLED DAMSON PLUMS

5 pounds fruit
3 pounds sugar
1 quart cider vinegar

2 ounces cloves
1 ounce cinnamon
½ ounce mace

Wash the fruit, drain and prick the plums with a long, sharp needle (an upholstery needle). Tie the spices in a small cheesecloth bag and tie loosely. Sprinkle sugar over fruit. Bring the cider vinegar and spices to a boil. Skim and pour over the fruit. Let stand 24 hours. Repeat the process three times. As the fruit and sugar will be cold, bring to the scalding point over very low heat; watch carefully before pouring the boiling hot vinegar over.

Remove the spice bag after the first or second boiling. Pour into stone crock and cover tightly. Keep in cool, dry place.

PLUM CONSERVE

18th century

4 pounds purple plums (Italian)	1 pound raisins
	3 pounds sugar
2 oranges, squeezed	½ cup water
1 lemon, squeezed	1 cup chopped nut meats

Rinse the fruit in cold water, drain, cut in half and remove the pits. Peel the oranges and lemon, scrape the thick white pith from the fruit, chop the rind very fine, add to the cut plums. They may be cut in quarters or put through a food grinder, as may the peel of the oranges and lemon. Add the sugar and water, stir until well mixed. Place over low heat and stir for a few minutes. Simmer at very low heat until well cooked and thick. Let cool slightly and add the nut meats. Pour into hot sterilized jars, cover with paraffin and store in a cool, dry place.

PRESERVED CHERRIES

4 pounds stoned red cherries   *3 pounds sugar*

Sprinkle half of the sugar over the cherries, and let stand
overnight. Simmer over very low heat, stirring frequently,
until the juice just comes to a boil. Pour the cherries into hot,
sterilized jars. Add the remaining sugar to the hot syrup and
cook until the syrup is very thick. Pour over the cherries in
the glass jars. Seal or cover with rounds of paper soaked in
brandy and tie down with string.

PRESERVED LEMON PEEL

For the best results, use an enamel kettle.

12 lemons   *Granulated sugar*

Cut lemons in half; extract juice. Then with a sharp knife,
scrape the lemon halves free of the white membrane. Cut
each half into thin strips, and cover with cold water. Bring
to boil, reduce heat to simmer and cook until the peel is
transparent.
Lift the strips from the water and drain on clean towel.
Pour the liquid into a bowl and set aside. Wash and dry the
kettle. Weigh the peel* and add an equal weight of sugar.
Cover with the same liquid and simmer over low heat until
the syrup is thick. Pour into small sterilized jars and cover
tightly.

* If a kitchen scales is not available, the store where you shop will
weigh the peel for you.

QUINCE PRESERVES

The season for fresh quinces is very short. Ask the store manager when the quince supply is expected.

Wash the skin thoroughly.

Cut the quinces into eighths. Core and remove any seeds. Peel and put all of the peelings into an enamel saucepan and cover with cold water. Simmer over low heat until the skins are soft. (An unpeeled sliced lemon will add a little needed flavor.)

Dampen a clean piece of cheesecloth. Strain the liquid and measure it.

To each cup of liquid, add one cup of sugar. Return to heat and stir until the sugar is dissolved. Allow to come to boiling point and add the slices of quince. Simmer over low heat until the fruit is tender.

Lift out carefully with slotted spoon or wire whisk. Place in hot sterilized jars. Cover with the syrup and cover tightly. If there is extra syrup, bottle it separately for fruit sauces next winter.

RED RASPBERRY JAM

Red raspberries   *Sugar*

Allow a pound of sugar to a pound of the berries. Rinse the berries carefully in cold water, a small quantity at a time. Lift out of the water with fingers or a slotted spoon. Drain on paper toweling. Mash the berries slightly with a *silver* fork. Simmer over very low heat for 15 minutes. Add the sugar and let it cook for 15 to 20 minutes. Pour a spoonful into a saucer. If it "jells" it is cooked enough. Pour into hot, sterilized jars. Cover tightly. This method makes a soft, tender jam.

SPICED GRAPES

Mrs. Steel's receipt—Delicious!

In many of the old cookbooks, and especially in the hand-written notebooks and the books compiled by various religious groups, the name of the contributor of each receipt was always listed. In one of the nineteenth-century Presbyterian Church cookbooks, a Mrs. Steel contributed this receipt for spiced grapes.

Wash bunches of Concord grapes, drain and slip pulp from skins. Simmer the pulp for ½ hour in small amount of water. Strain through coarse sieve. Simmer the skins separately in small amount of water until tender.

Combine the strained pulp and the skins. Measure accurately and add sugar in equal quantity. To every three quarts of mixture add 2 teaspoons each: ground cloves, cinnamon, allspice.

Stir thoroughly, place over low heat in deep enamel kettle and simmer until very thick, stirring occasionally. Seal and cover tightly with paraffin.

TUTTI-FRUTTI

This delicacy deserves to be returned to the modern cook's repertoire, even though it involves considerable care and effort. Its origin has been traced to France where it was known as a Melange of Fruit, and its preparation was very complicated and elaborate.

From France the receipt crossed into Holland, where it received the more prosaic name of Dutch Fruit Salad. From there the receipt came across the Atlantic where it was dubbed Tutti-Frutti and is still known by that name today. Whatever its name, Tutti-Frutti is a melange of fruits and berries, sweetened and put down in an earthenware crock, and liberally laced with *good* brandy.

How to Prepare Tutti-Frutti Today

Sterilize a large crock with boiling water. Dry it thoroughly and let stand in the sunshine. Tie in a small cheesecloth bag: whole cloves, stick cinnamon, allspice, lemon and orange peel. Wash, dry and crush the strawberries. Add the sugar in equal amounts, and the bag of spices.

Simmer over low heat until the berries are soft. Remove the spices and pour the mixture into a flannel jelly bag and let hang from a hook over a large bowl until the liquid has dripped through. Add 1 pint brandy, pour into the crock, cover tightly and keep in a cool, dark place for one week.

Then as the summer progresses, add a layer of any fresh fruit, washed, drained and mixed with an equal amount of sugar. (Never add more than two quarts of fruit at a single time.) Always add one pint of brandy with each additional quantity of fruit. Stir thoroughly with each addition.

Red Tutti-Frutti

Use the red fruits and berries only: cherries, strawberries, red raspberries, red plums. This is a very handsome sauce to be served with ice cream. Plain blanc mange is enhanced by a spoonful of the tutti-frutti; so are plain puddings.

If a cool, dark cellar is not available, when the harvest is over, pour the sauce into hot, sterilized jars and cover tightly. If there is a generous amount of syrup, store separately in the hot sterilized jars.

Invalid Cookery

In the days of harsher living, the writers of cookbooks gave special attention to dishes especially prepared for the sick. Great emphasis was placed on the "wholesomeness" of the foods given to an invalid. One writer noted that "sponge cake is an excellent lunch for an invalid, as it contains wholesome eggs, milk and sugar."

Another writer stated that "if the patient's condition permits, allow them to have plain, wholesome food. but with the weak and debilitated, the delicacies must take their place; and I desire to call special attention to, and to give my sanction and advice; that if any special thing is craved, be it food or drink, I would most positively allow it, in moderation . . . there has recently come to my knowledge the case of a patient who was saved (his life) by drinking two quarts of hard cider. And when he got hold of the pitcher he would not let go until it was empty. . . . I do not call this, however, 'in moderation.' " But he was stronger than the nurse, the writer concludes.

CHOCOLATE CREAM

2 tablespoons sugar
1 oz. unsweetened chocolate,
   melted
1 pint table cream

4 egg whites, stiffly beaten
¼ teaspoon salt
1 teaspoon vanilla extract

Simmer the chocolate, sugar and cream over low heat until cream is scalded, stirring constantly. Set aside to cool, add the egg whites, salt and flavoring. Fold in the whites until all pieces are absorbed. Fill parfait glasses, and serve very cold.

COFFEE JELLY

This is a variation of Velvet Cream. Omit the sherry wine and the lemon juice. Substitute ½ cup very strong coffee, boiling hot. Pour over the softened gelatine.

PUNCHEON JELLY

1 tablespoon unflavored
   gelatin
1 cup cold water
½ cup strong hot tea

½ cup sugar
¼ cup rum
1 tablespoon brandy

Sprinkle the gelatine over the cold water, add the tea and stir until the gelatine is dissolved. Add the sugar, rum and brandy. Stir until the sugar is dissolved. Let stand until thick and syrupy. Pour into pretty glasses. Top with cream flavored with powdered sugar and brandy.

   * Strain all jellies prepared with gelatine.

AN EGGNOG FOR THE SICK

This is palatable and for weak patients will be found very invigorating and strengthening, the true 'Madeira' being rich in its tonic and invigorating qualities.

1 egg yolk
1 tablespoon powdered sugar
1 tablespoon brandy
2 tablespoons Madeira wine

1 cup milk (*very cold*)
Grated nutmeg
1 egg white, stiffly beaten

Beat the egg yolk with the sugar to the consistency of cream; add brandy, wine, milk and a sprinkling of nutmeg. Fold in the egg white. Pour into a very tall glass.

PEACH FOAM

4 tree-ripened peaches
½ cup powdered sugar

1 egg white

Peel and stone peaches. Beat with a fork for half an hour when it will be a thick, perfectly smooth velvety cream, with a delightful peach flavor.

SNOW PUDDING

It should be perfect, white, literally like snow.

1 tablespoon unflavored gelatine
¼ cup cold water
1 cup boiling water

1 cup sugar
¼ cup lemon juice
3 egg whites, stiffly beaten

Sprinkle the gelatine over the cold water. Add the boiling water, sugar and lemon juice. Stir until sugar is dissolved. Strain and set aside until thick and syrupy. It must be completely cold before the egg whites are added. Add the whites and stir slowly until the mixture is a smooth mass.

Serve with a soft custard sauce made from the egg yolks p. 225).

VELVET CREAM

This dessert derives its name from its smooth consistency.

1 tablespoon unflavored gelatin	½ cup sugar
	whipping:
¼ cup cold water	1½ cups cream
¼ cup sherry wine	⅛ teaspoon salt
1 teaspoon lemon juice	

Sprinkle gelatine over cold water, add the wine and stir over hot water until the gelatine is dissolved. Add the lemon juice and sugar. Stir until sugar is dissolved. Strain through a fine sieve or a piece of clean, dampened cheesecloth. Set aside until thick and syrupy but not "set." Pour in the cream and stir until well blended. As soon as it thickens, pour into pretty glasses.

WINE JELLY

1 tablespoon unflavored gelatine	1-inch stick cinnamon
	2 or 3 whole cloves
¼ cup cold water	½ cup sugar
1¼ cups boiling water	½ cup sherry wine

Sprinkle the gelatine over the cold water.
Simmer the water, spices and sugar over low heat until syrupy. Strain out the spices and pour the liquid over the gelatine, stir well and add the wine. Strain and set aside to chill. Pour into glass bowl or individual glasses.
Serve with cream.

Variation
For a true lemon flavor, omit the spices and add juice of one-half lemon.